"This little book is an empowering guide. It sets out a clear way for young people (and others) to hold governments and corporations to account for failures to take the climate crisis seriously. This powerful little book breaks new ground, offering a cost-free, barrier-free tool for activism. I highly recommend it! Go, set up a youth climate court, call power to account using this unique way of taking action. Do it everywhere."

Anna Grear, *Founder and first Director of the Global Network for the Study of Human Rights and the Environment, and Professor of Law at Cardiff University, UK*

T0386464

Youth Climate Courts

This book focuses on Youth Climate Courts, a bold new tool that young people in their teens and twenties can use to compel their local city or county government to live up to its human rights obligations, formally acknowledge the climate crisis, and take major steps to address it.

Tom Kerns shows how youth climate leaders can form their own local Youth Climate Court, with youth judges, youth prosecuting attorneys, and youth jury members, and put their local city or county government on trial for not meeting its human rights obligations. Kerns describes how a Youth Climate Court works, how to start one, what human rights are, what they require of local governments, and what governmental changes a Youth Climate Court can realistically hope to accomplish. The book offers young activists a brand new, user-friendly, cost-free, barrier-free, powerful tool for forcing local governments to come to terms with their obligation to protect the rights of their citizens with respect to the climate crisis.

This book offers a unique new tool to young climate activists hungry for genuinely effective ways to directly move governments to aggressively address the climate crisis.

Tom Kerns is Director of Environment and Human Rights Advisory and Professor Emeritus of Philosophy at North Seattle College, USA. His work brings human rights norms to bear on environmental issues, especially on the climate crisis. In 2015 he served on the drafting group for the international "Declaration on Human Rights and Climate Change," and from 2014 until 2018 he co-organized the 2018 Permanent Peoples' Tribunal Session on Human Rights, Fracking and Climate Change. He is co-editor, with Kathleen Dean Moore, of *Bearing Witness: The Human Rights Case Against Fracking and Climate Change* (2021), a book based on the testimony and findings in that Tribunal.

Youth Climate Courts
How You Can Host a Human Rights
Trial for People and Planet

Thomas A. Kerns

Routledge
Taylor & Francis Group
LONDON AND NEW YORK

from Routledge

First published 2022
by Routledge
2 Park Square, Milton Park, Abingdon, Oxon OX14 4RN

and by Routledge
605 Third Avenue, New York, NY 10158

Routledge is an imprint of the Taylor & Francis Group, an informa business

© 2022 Thomas A. Kerns

British Library Cataloguing-in-Publication Data
A catalogue record for this book is available from the British Library

Library of Congress Cataloging-in-Publication Data
Names: Kerns, Thomas A., 1942– author.
Title: Youth climate courts: how you can host a human rights trial for people and planet / Thomas A. Kerns.
Description: Abingdon, Oxon; New York, NY: Routledge, 2022. | Includes bibliographical references. |
Contents: Dear reader – Introduction – How does a youth climate court work – What are human rights? – Which specific human rights? – CODA: Youth interventions for an addicted world.
Identifiers: LCCN 2021031290 (print) | LCCN 2021031291 (ebook) | ISBN 9781032109091 (hardback) | ISBN 9781032109060 (paperback) | ISBN 9781003217640 (ebook)
Subjects: LCSH: Climatic changes–Law and legislation–Juvenile literature. | Climatic changes–Government policy–Youth participation–Juvenile literature. | Mock trials–Juvenile literature.
Classification: LCC K3585.5 . K47 2022 (print) | LCC K3585.5 (ebook) | DDC 344.04/633–dc23
LC record available at https://lccn.loc.gov/2021031290
LC ebook record available at https://lccn.loc.gov/2021031291

ISBN: 978-1-032-10909-1 (hbk)
ISBN: 978-1-032-10906-0 (pbk)
ISBN: 978-1-003-21764-0 (ebk)

DOI: 10.4324/9781003217640

Typeset in Bembo
by Newgen Publishing UK

For my grandchildren, Kate, Robin, Orion, Cassie, and Tyler, and for their children and children's children and all the young ones to come.

Contents

Acknowledgments

Preparing any book, even a short one like this, happens only with help and input from many good people. To everyone who has contributed to this book, knowingly or unknowingly, I send respect and deep gratitude for your contributions to this project and to the world. Thank you especially:

- To Emily Grubby, copy editor extraordinaire, who really *gets* what this little book is about, who *gets* the intimate connections between human rights and the climate breakdown, and who really *gets* what human rights are and why they are the perfect foundation for Youth Climate Courts. Thank you, Emily, for your insight, for your sensitive attention to the book's feel and tone, and for your good sense of the right order in which sentences and paragraphs should appear. Also for your eerie ability to spot out-of-place commas, colons, and tiny dashes. This manuscript has benefitted enormously from your commitment, your caring, your attention to detail, and your well-tuned sense of good argument and good order.
- To Kathleen Dean Moore, for your generous and ongoing encouragement in our work together these past few years, for bringing together the Spring Creek Project and the Permanent Peoples' Tribunal Session on Human Rights, Fracking and Climate Change, thus setting the stage for that Tribunal's important work. Thank you especially for your invitation to work together on the book about that Tribunal, *Bearing Witness: The Human Rights Case Against Fracking and Climate Change*, which provided the groundwork for this Youth Climate Courts book. This Youth Climate Courts book would not have come to be, and certainly not in its present form, without your generous encouragement, suggestions, and time.
- To Anna Grear, for the raw enjoyment of working with you as co-imaginer, co-initiator, and co-organizer of the Permanent Peoples'

Tribunal Session on Human Rights, Fracking and Climate Change and for the creative energy and rich flow of ideas that have sprung from our collaborations on that, on the Declaration on Human Rights and Climate Change, and on so much else. Your courageous and contagious creativity has led directly to imagining Youth Climate Courts into existence.

- To Maura Stephens and your team, for your enthusiastic encouragement of the Youth Climate Courts project, of this book, and of those high school students planning their own trial.
- To Lisa Millstein, for your generous engagement with YouthClimateCourts.org as its Legal Fellow, for your much-appreciated support of Youth Climate Court organizers, and for your editorial suggestions that have helped improve this book.
- To Tom Kerns and Lisa Gray, the extraordinary brother-sister website development team that created the truly eye-catching, beautifully organized much-praised youthclimatecourts.org website. Thank you too, from your proud and admiring father, for all your help brainstorming and organizing the website, keeping it updated, and making the newsletter and social media work so smoothly.
- To Professor Judith Preston and her law students who, inspired by the Youth Climate Courts idea, testified before The Land and Environment Court in Sydney, Australia, Chief Judge Brian Preston presiding, giving the world its first taste of what Youth Climate Courts would become.
- To the courageous young high school women organizing the first Youth Climate Court trial to be conducted in the US. You know who you are.

Dear reader

If you are a young person who would like to get together with a few friends, declare yourselves to be a Youth Climate Court, and then put your city or county government on trial for not doing enough to protect your human rights to health, to security of person, and to a stable and sustainable climate system, then this book is for you.

City and county governments that are not adequately addressing the climate crisis need to be called to account for failing to protect the basic human rights of their citizens. Who better to do this than the very people, young people, whose lives and rights are being, and will continue to be, most dramatically undermined?

Youth Climate Courts are youth-initiated, youth-led, youth-organized, and youth-conducted. They select a youth judge, a youth prosecuting attorney, and youth jury members. The Youth Climate Court then organizes a trial. The Court issues a summons to the local government to designate an elected official who will attend court proceedings and explain the government's position in open Youth Court. The charges will be that the government is not living up to its human rights obligations. The youth prosecutor will argue that the government is failing to adequately protect the basic human rights of its citizens, especially its children, in the face of clear and present threats from the climate crisis.

If that sounds like a promising approach, a new, bold, and powerful way for young people to compel their local governments to act, then this book describes exactly how to do that.

The book's argument is pretty simple. It goes like this:

1   The primary obligation of a government is to protect the rights of its citizens (the US Declaration of Independence, for example, says that people are created equal and have certain basic rights, and that "to secure these rights governments are instituted among men"[1]).

Recognition of that primary responsibility of governments is central to this book.

2   Catastrophic climate change threatens to undermine many of those rights and may ultimately threaten all of them.

3   Young people have the most to lose in the face of the climate crisis, so you need a strong platform from which to speak truth to governments, especially to those governments that have so far failed to listen.

4   Rather than just waiting around for governments to act, young people can take the initiative yourselves, declare yourselves to be a Youth Climate Court and then put your local government on trial for failing to secure its citizens' rights to life, to health, to water, and to a healthy, sustainable environment. Young people can thus pressure local governments to reflect on what they have done and not done, and to carefully consider what they should now be doing.

5   If the Youth Climate Court jury finds the local government guilty of failing in its primary obligation as a government – to protect its citizens' rights – the Youth Court will issue one or more formal mandates to that government, such as requiring it to (1) formally declare a climate emergency and (2) develop a science-based, human-rights-respecting Climate Action Plan by a certain date and submit it back to the Youth Court for approval.

This book describes how a Youth Climate Court works, how to start one, what human rights are and what they require of governments, what the Youth Court can do, and the effects on local governments it can hope to accomplish.

Besides a Youth Climate Court's benefits for local governments (more on this later) and its benefits in fighting the climate crisis, the experience of organizing and conducting a Youth Climate Court trial will also have benefits for the young people who take on this work. They will

- make a real difference in the world;
- learn how courts work;
- learn how local governments work;
- learn about the power of human rights and how they differ from ordinary laws;
- learn how to plan out a persuasive argument and present it publicly;
- learn how to organize a team-based creative project;
- gain experience in how to interact with government officials;
- help fight the climate crisis;
- enjoy working on an important and worthwhile project with friends.

That adds up to a lot of valuable learning. If this project were done as an independent study project it could earn academic credit and service-learning credit as well.

Youth Climate Courts offer a bold opportunity for young people to make a genuine difference in the world and to effect real change in real government policies. While this work is challenging, there is certainly no one better poised to take it on. Young people who do this work will affect lives throughout their community and for many generations to come.

Note

1 *US Declaration of Independence*: "We hold these truths to be self-evident, that all men are created equal, that they are endowed by their Creator with certain unalienable Rights, that among these are Life, Liberty and the pursuit of Happiness. That to secure these rights, Governments are instituted among Men, deriving their just powers from the consent of the governed, That whenever any Form of Government becomes destructive of these ends, it is the Right of the People to alter or to abolish it, and to institute new Government, laying its foundation on such principles and organizing its powers in such form, as to them shall seem most likely to effect their Safety and Happiness." www.archives.gov/founding-docs/declaration-transcript.

Introduction

Premises

The premises of this book are simple, clear, and obvious:

1   Young people are those most affected by the climate crisis and the younger they are, the more dramatically their lives will be impacted. They will live with it during their most vulnerable and formative years, and they will live with it longer as Earth's climate continues to worsen. When governments fail to act, young people are the ones most grievously wronged by that failure.
2   Further, many young people cannot vote, cannot run for elective office, have no formal voice in public affairs, and certainly no power in the councils of government where decisions about Earth's future, and theirs, are being made (or not made, or perhaps not even considered).
3   Since governments are unlikely to grant decision-making powers to them any time soon, if young people are to have power, they will need to take it and exercise it themselves, using human rights methods readily available in ordinary civil society. Anyone can do this.

This book outlines a bold, creative new opportunity, a new way for young people to step forward, voice their truth publicly, and exercise real power to effect real change in real governments. It describes what a Youth Climate Court is, how to organize one for yourself, and how to conduct your own trial. It describes how Youth Climate Court trials can benefit local governments and help them address the climate crisis. The Youth Climate Courts described here will offer young people in their teens and twenties all around the world one more way to use their powerful voices, their persuasive moral urgency, and the strength they may not yet realize

DOI: 10.4324/9781003217640-1

they possess to work cooperatively with, and exert real pressure on, their local governments to effect real change.

The idea for Youth Climate Courts grew out of the great success of the Permanent Peoples'Tribunal Session on Human Rights, Fracking and Climate Change[1] that was organized over several years and brought to the Permanent Peoples' Tribunal (PPT) in Rome for a series of hearings in 2018. The Permanent Peoples'Tribunal was chosen because of its status as a highly respected international, civil society, human rights court. Four preliminary tribunals had been organized by local leaders in Youngstown, Ohio; Athens, Ohio; Charlottesville, Virginia; and in Brisbane, Australia, leading up to the week-long plenary session of the PPT in May of 2018. Ten PPT judges heard hundreds of witnesses from all over the world, listened to arguments and testimony from more than a dozen attorneys, studied *amicus curiae* briefs from leaders of prominent non-governmental organizations, examined United Nations reports, and much more. Fifteen prominent thought leaders from across the United States contributed to the weekly Bedrock Lecture Series[2] that led up to the Tribunal's plenary session, and their lectures were also submitted to the court as testimony. The court was asked for an advisory opinion[3] on four formal questions[4] and the judges issued their advisory opinion in early 2019.[5] A book based on that Tribunal, edited by Thomas Kerns and Kathleen Dean Moore, is titled *Bearing Witness: The Human Rights Case Against Fracking and Climate Change*.[6] It was the great success of that Tribunal and of the court's powerful advisory opinion and recommendations that laid the ground-work for these Youth Climate Courts.

The Youth Climate Courts model thus grew, on the one hand, from the success of that Tribunal and, on the other, from a deep concern for the well-being of young people around the world and for the frustration and hopelessness many of them feel. They have, after all, no available avenues of power to force their governments to wake up, to make them take the climate crisis seriously, and then to compel them to act.

The plight of the young

It is certainly understandable why young people would feel discouraged and anxious when seeing how slow the adult world has been to recognize the severity of this problem and how little has yet been done by most governments. As Oregon Health and Science University Professor David Pollack has said, many people, especially young children, are already experiencing "eco-anxiety."

"They are frightened, and they have good reason to be. They didn't ask for this, they didn't contribute to the problem, but it's there and it's in their laps and laps of future generations," Pollack said. "It is already leading to various kinds of symptoms and problems that people are having with hopelessness, escapist behavior, anger, and even decisions to not have children."[7]

These concerns were evident during the COP25 meetings in Madrid, Spain in late 2019. Thousands of young people marched in the streets carrying banners, some clever like "Merry Crisis and a Happy New Fear" and some darker and more insistent like, "You Will Die of Old Age, I Will Die of Climate Change."[8]

Given these entirely understandable feelings, what can be done? *New York Times* environmental author Emma Marris thinks that *doing* something, taking on a project, any project, can be a big help. "I firmly believe that doing something is the 'cure' for 'eco-anxiety,'" she said.

And while doing something may feel a little bit hard at first, you might find — as I have — that when you do it with others who have the same fears and the same great love for the world, that the anxiety recedes like a tide. In its place, you may feel a calm determination and even something strangely like joy.[9]

For young people casting about for something to do, Youth Climate Courts provide a brand-new option. There are, of course, many other creative and engaging ways for young people to express their concerns about the climate crisis too, so when a young person is trying to decide which of those actions to engage with, it can be overwhelming. There is no way to predict which approaches will be the most successful. What can be known in advance, though, is which approaches feel most personally appealing, which feel most enlivening, which promise some degree of hope and agency, and which a person is drawn to take on, engage with, and give their energies to. Youth Climate Courts and the public trials they conduct are a brand-new approach available to young people. This little book outlines the purposes, background, and methods involved in forming a Youth Climate Court, and outlines steps for how to do it.

It is certainly true that young people are the ones with the most to lose in this crisis. They are the ones with the most at stake, and they know it. The crisis is affecting them now, and more so every year, and it will continue to affect the life choices they will be making in the coming years and decades of their lives. They understand clearly that "The existential issue of climate puts everyone at risk, but the younger you are, the greater the stakes."[10]

They also know that it is the policies, choices and practices created and carried out by the past few human generations that have caused the problem. People now in their teens and twenties, many still in school and many still living with their parents, are not the human cohort primarily responsible for having created the policies and practices that govern today's world. It was instead today's adults and their forebears. It was they who went along with, who lived in and lived *by*, the social mechanisms, value structures, economic incentives, and the worldview of today's developed industrialized societies.

It is no wonder young people feel discouraged, depressed, frustrated, and helpless. It is no wonder they feel voiceless and agency-less, no wonder that they feel as if they have no power to do anything about a situation that will affect them so dramatically for the rest of their lives. They have instead had to rely on adults and those adults have, at least so far, not evidenced much initiative in facing up to and taking on the climate crisis.

Climate reports from the Intergovernmental Panel on Climate Change (IPCC), from the United Nations, from the World Health Organization[11] and other intergovernmental agencies, as well as from civil society organizations around the world have made clear for years now that the global situation is dire and becoming more dire each year. Media reports show greenhouse gas emissions continuing to rise every year, despite national commitments agreed to in the 2016 Paris Accords. Governments daily are failing to take adequate steps to address the increasingly ominous and increasingly inevitable predictions.

As those young people marched in the streets of Madrid during the COP25 climate summit, in one conference room inside one building, the first slide in a PowerPoint presentation was asking "How do we empower young people in climate activism?"[12]

The Youth Climate Courts described in this book offer one clear and powerful way to empower young leaders to grab the reins, to speak their truth out loud and publicly, and to effectively exercise the formidable moral power they are now discovering is at their disposal.

Brief overview of Youth Climate Courts

If local governments – primarily cities and counties, but also school districts and other special districts – are failing to adequately address the climate crisis, then Youth Climate Courts can provide youth leaders both voice and agency. Youth Courts can provide a platform from which to speak their truth publicly, reasonably, and passionately, and provide also a measure of actual moral power to compel their local governments to take those concerns seriously and act on them.

A Youth Climate Court is created by young people themselves. Any trial the Youth Court conducts will have a youth judge, a youth prosecuting attorney, and youth jury members. The Youth Court will put its city, county, or other local government publicly on trial for failing to do what it long ago should have been doing to address the climate crisis.

Governments are clearly the primary institutions in societies for creating policies, social strategies, guidelines, ordinances, and laws. They are the entities whose job is to deliberate, listen to their citizens, enact new laws and policies, and enforce them. So governments are the entities we turn to when societies need to make changes, especially big changes. Young people already know how to organize protest marches, Fridays for Future demonstrations, and other forms of action to catch the attention of governments and make them do something about the climate crisis. Valuable as these forms of protest have been and will continue to be, a Youth Climate Court trial has real advantages too. It can grab a government's attention boldly and pointedly and in a manner that is much harder for a government to ignore, partly because the trial they organize puts that local government squarely in the dock, and partly because the Youth Court metaphorically points a finger directly at that government and says, out loud and publicly, "j'accuse." How could a local government not notice that? And how could they not, even if only quietly and privately to themselves, recognize and appreciate the pressure young people are putting on them to do what they already know they should be doing but simply have not done.

One advantage of the Youth Climate Courts approach is that it embodies many of the strengths and virtues of actual governmental court proceedings. A Youth Climate Court trial, for example, is a serious and dignified proceeding. It takes place in a kind of courtroom which, like government courtrooms, is a place set apart, a place characterized by decorum, by respect for the law, respect for the opposing parties and respect for the process. It is, moreover, dedicated to reasoned argument, to truth-telling, and to clear standards of law and conduct. Its arguments rely on solid, science-based testimony and personal-narrative testimony and they are grounded in well-established human rights norms and law. In the United States they are based too on principles expressed in the US Declaration of Independence and in the US Constitution and Bill of Rights. Courtrooms, furthermore, as organs of the third, judicial, non-political branch of governments, are expected to rise above appeals to partisan politics and to instead follow the norms of law. All these characteristics give Youth Climate Court trials a sense of weight, dignity and gravitas that will be difficult for city councils and county boards of commissioners to ignore.

Another key advantage of the Youth Climate Courts approach is that it is based in human rights standards and laws, and that it puts pressure on democratically elected governments (rather than on corporations or other private entities) to live up to and respect the human rights protections they are required to secure for their citizens. This approach insists that governments meet the human rights obligations they properly bear.

Finally, another big advantage of this Youth Climate Courts approach is that it applies its pressures from the bottom-up, rather than from the top-down, in these four ways: (1) it starts with young people rather than with adults, that is, with people at the bottom of the power structures rather than with people at the top, (2) it is a grass roots, community-based effort, starting in local communities and working with local community members and local officials, (3) it works with governments that are smaller, local, and more accessible rather than with governments at the state, provincial, or federal level which are more remote, much larger, more complex, and can often feel opaque and inaccessible. Further, (4) this approach appeals to human rights standards which are themselves, as we will see in Chapter 2, also a bottom-up approach. Human rights standards appeal to governments from the perspective of ordinary people whose rights governments are obliged to protect, and whose rights must be protected if they are to live even a minimally decent life. More on this in Chapter 2 when we examine exactly what human rights are, how they arise, and what they mean for regular people.

We have seen that the Youth Climate Court process provides a platform for young people to speak truth to power. It accomplishes this through the arguments presented by the Court's prosecuting attorneys, the verdict of its jury, and the strength of the publicity leading up to and following the trial. The Youth Court's agency is exercised (1) when the Court persuades the government to appear in the courtroom to defend its actions, (2) when the Court garners media coverage reporting on the trial, (3) when the Youth Court issues a mandate requiring the government to declare a climate emergency, develop a Climate Action Plan, enter into a restorative justice process with the Youth Court, or any of the other mandates it may issue, (4) when young people keep the pressure on the government to ensure that the mandates get completed on time, and (5) when the Youth Climate Court organizers record and report on their experience to the International Coalition of Youth Courts where it will be archived for use by future Youth Climate Court organizers.

Creating a Youth Climate Court and putting a local city or county government on trial may sound unusual, perhaps even improper, and certainly bold to some people. But if governments are failing to act, failing in their duty to protect the rights of their citizens, especially of their children, then it will be those young citizens who are best placed to publicly call those governments to account.

Further, lest there be any doubt that the voices of young people can have power, remember Malala Yousafzai who, at age 15, had been an active advocate in Pakistan for the education of girls and later was awarded the Nobel Peace Prize in 2014, the youngest Nobel laureate ever.[13] Severn Suzuki was only 12 years old when she spoke to the United Nations Plenary Session at the Earth Summit in Rio de Janeiro in 1992,[14] Xiuhtezcatl Martinez was only 15 when he delivered a speech on climate change to the United Nations,[15] and Greta Thunberg was just 15 when she first began her Fridays for Climate sessions outside the Parliament House in Stockholm, Sweden in 2018.

Note also what Mary Robinson, former president of Ireland and former United Nations High Commissioner for Human Rights, told the audience in a speech at Boston College in 2019.

> She said that she knows someone who is the head of a fossil fuel company – Robinson didn't name him – who has finally decided to do something about the damage his firm has caused. The impetus? His teenage daughter, who, according to Robinson told him: "Daddy, you are responsible for destroying this world."[16]

As that father listened to his daughter, so other adults must, and will, attend to what their children are telling them because it is children's present and future lives that are being threatened by the failures of adult institutions to act.

Purposes of Youth Climate Courts

When youth leaders set out to organize their Youth Climate Court trial, they will want to keep in mind which specific purposes they want their project to accomplish. Some possible goals on which organizers might choose to focus are listed here, and local organizers may wish to add others. Having a clear idea of the goals at which they are aiming can help organizers stay focused on the outcomes that are most important to them. Possible goals:

1 To provide young people another powerful way to speak their truth, exercise their agency, and compel their governments to change.
2 To publicly and forcibly grab the attention of a local government.
3 To ultimately persuade the local government to take serious action on the climate crisis.
4 To show support for elected officials who are working to enact climate policies and climate legislation.

5   To garner public support for legal cases around the world, such as *Juliana v. United States, LaRose v. Her Majesty the Queen in Canada*, and many others.[17]

6   To pave the way for future, official court actions against local governments that fail to meet their human rights obligations with respect to the climate crisis.

7   To learn about human rights, to remind governments of their human rights obligations, and to show governments how human rights norms bear directly on the climate crisis.

8   To enjoy working together with friends on an important project of genuinely global significance.

The book proceeds in this way:

Chapter 1 describes the simple, easy steps for creating a Court and describes how to put a local government on trial. It lays out how the Court will summon leaders of the government to appear before the Youth Court to explain and defend themselves. It explains that the charges will be that the government is failing to adequately protect the human rights of its citizens, especially of the children.

It describes how, on the appointed day, the young judge will call the court to order, the young prosecuting attorney (or prosecuting team) will argue that the city or county government has failed to meet its obligation to protect the rights of its citizens, and will perhaps call witnesses to support that argument. At that point the government representative may wish to argue that the government *has* taken effective measures to prepare for and protect against the effects of climate change and to protect the rights of its citizens. Or, more likely, the government representative may simply acknowledge that the government just has not yet done enough. After the youth prosecutor and the defendant government's representative have completed their initial arguments and their closing arguments, the youth jury retires to the jury room to discuss what it has heard and to render its judgment.

If the government is found guilty of failing to protect community members' rights, the Youth Climate Court "retains jurisdiction" and issues one or more mandates to the government, requiring it to complete them by a certain date. Mandates could include requiring the government to formally declare a climate emergency, requiring the government to prepare a comprehensive, science-based, human rights-respecting Climate Action Plan and submitted it to the Youth Court for approval, or requiring the government to complete any of the other possible mandates suggested toward the end of Chapter 1. Then, in the weeks and months following the trial, Youth Court members keep pressure on that government to complete its mandates before the court-imposed deadline. Youth Court members may hold demonstrations, engage with local media, attend city council meetings or county board of commissioners' meetings, and generally keep up the pressure until the mandates have been completed and reported back to the Youth Court.

Chapter 1 also describes what a trial's outcomes can be and what mandates can subsequently be required of the government that has been put on trial.

Chapter 2 explains what human rights are, where they come from, why they are such important and powerful norms, why governments are obliged to respect, protect and fulfill them for their citizens, and why they are the perfect central core and legal grounding for these Youth Climate Court trials.

Chapter 3 describes a number of specific human rights norms that are put at clear risk by the climate crisis, some of which Youth Court prosecutors may wish to highlight when planning their arguments. It describes what each of those rights means, how and why each right is especially relevant to the climate crisis, and in which human rights declarations and covenants that particular right has been recognized and declared.

One note of clarification: The Youth Climate Courts described in this book are not the same as, nor do they have the same level of judicial authority as, those formal legal actions being heard in federal, provincial, and state government courts around the world, such as the suits brought by the team at Our Children's Trust (OCT) in Eugene, Oregon. In OCT's most famous case, *Juliana v. United States*, a group of 21 youth plaintiffs from around the US are suing the US government in federal court for climate-damaging actions and policies that the government has knowingly and affirmatively implemented over the decades that have resulted in undermining a wide range of human and constitutional rights. This case has been considered by many the most important court action in the world right now.

Juliana v. United States, often referred to as *Youth v Gov*,[18] may be OCT's most prominent case right now but it is certainly not their only one. The Our Children's Trust attorneys have open cases in many US states and in several countries around the world.[19] All those cases are pressing the courts to recognize the special peril that the climate crisis holds for young people. These cases and others like them are formal, legal cases brought before government-based courts at the state, federal, and international levels. The rulings of these courts can be enforced by the various compulsory powers available to governments, but not available to civil society organizations like YouthClimateCourts.org.

The Youth Climate Courts that are the subject of this book are different. They are certainly inspired by the vision, stamina, and commitment of the hard-working people bringing those cases, but these Youth Climate Courts are not formal government courts. They are local, one-time, civil society,[20] court trials created in a specific location by a self-chosen team of young leaders who need a platform, a megaphone, to express their concerns. Youth Climate Courts offer young people a measure of power and agency, and help them move governments to make the changes that should have been made long ago.

And yet, different as Youth Climate Courts are from the official litigation described above, the two kinds of work are still, at least in some respects, parallel and mutually beneficial. There are important ways in which each can be of use to the other. Youth Climate Courts can certainly learn from the official federal, state, and provincial cases underway around the world. They can learn how those cases are structured and argued and what elements of the evidence and arguments are most salient. In turn, from the other side, Youth Climate Court trials can help build public support and enthusiasm for the critically important, rights-based climate cases brought by Our Children's Trust and others.

How to read this book

The book can be read in any order you like. If you would like to start directly with the practical steps for forming a Youth Climate Court, just start with Chapter 1: How does a Youth Climate Court work? If you would like to see some specific human rights that are put at risk by climate change, check out Chapter 3: Which specific human rights? If you would like to get a feel for what human rights are, how they form the basis of Youth Climate Court trials, how the modern human rights movement came to be, and why human rights are such an important and powerful (perhaps even necessary) tool for addressing the climate crisis, you can begin with Chapter 2: What are human rights? In other words, just turn to whichever chapters grab your attention and start the book from there.

If you use this book to develop a Youth Climate Court of your own, or if you just want to explore the ideas in the book with others, you will probably discover that others who have read it noticed, underlined, or focused on different ideas and themes than you did. Because of that, your understanding of these ideas can be deeply enriched by meeting and talking about the book with others who have read it too.

Notes

1 www.tribunalonfracking.org/.
2 www.tribunalonfracking.org/bedrock-lectures/.

3 www.tribunalonfracking.org/judges-statements/.

4 www.tribunalonfracking.org/what-is-this-session-about/.

5 www.tribunalonfracking.org/judges-statements/.

6 Available from Oregon State University Press, April 2021. www.osupress. oregonstate.edu/book/bearing-witness.

7 Oregon Public Broadcasting, Oregon Call to Action on Climate, Health and Equity, 2-5-20 www.oregonpublichealth.org/assets/Oregon%20CALL%20 TO%20ACTION.pdf (accessed 2-15-20).

8 *Time Magazine*, 12-23-19. https://time.com/person-of-the-year-2019-greta-thunberg/. The *Time Magazine* article mentions clever banners from marches in other cities around the world: "In London: The World is Hotter than Young Leonardo DiCaprio. In Turkey: Every Disaster Movie Starts with a Scientist Being Ignored. In New York: The Dinosaurs Thought They Had Time, Too."

9 Emma Marris, "Here's What It Was Like to Get Arrested During an Environmental Protest," *Sierra*, 12-7-19. www.sierraclub.org/sierra/here-s-what-it-was-get-arrested-during-environmental-protest (accessed 1-14-20).

10 *Time Magazine*, 12-23-19. https://time.com/person-of-the-year-2019-greta-thunberg/.

11 www.who.int/health-topics/climate-change#tab=tab_1.

12 *Time Magazine*, 12-23-19. https://time.com/person-of-the-year-2019-greta-thunberg/.

13 Malala Yousafzai, *I Am Malala: How One Girl Stood Up for Education and Changed the World* (Young Readers Edition). New York: Little, Brown Books for Young Readers, 2016.

14 www.youtube.com/watch?v=TQmz6Rbpnu0&feature=youtu.be.

15 https://en.wikipedia.org/wiki/Xiuhtezcatl_Martinez.

16 Robinson, Mary, in a speech at Boston College on 11-11-19. www.ncronline. org/news/earthbeat/mary-robinson-disruption-best-option-left-head-climate-disaster (accessed 1-25-20).

17 www.ourchildrenstrust.org/juliana-v-us (accessed 10-20-20). Other rights-based climate cases have been successfully decided in, for example, the 2018 decision of the Colombian Supreme Court www.dejusticia.org/en/climate-change-and-future-generations-lawsuit-in-colombia-key-excerpts-from-the-supreme-courts-decision/ (accessed 12-31-20), and the 2019 Urgenda decision from the Dutch Supreme Court www.climatedocket.com/2019/ 12/20/urgenda-climate-ruling-netherlands-supreme-court/ (accessed 12-31-20). Other cases are also underway in courts in Brazil and Norway, and in international institutions like the European Court of Human Rights, the United Nations Human Rights Committee, and the United Nations Committee on the Rights of the Child. Youth Climate Courts can help provide public support for cases such as these.

18 See www.youthvgov.org.

19 www.ourchildrenstrust.org/juliana-v-us (accessed 10-20-20).

20 The term "civil society" just refers to individuals, non-governmental organizations (NGOs), and other self-forming sections of society that are independent of the government.

The United Nations defines "civil society" as the third sector of society, "along with government and business. It comprises civil society organizations and non-governmental organizations. The UN recognizes the importance of partnering with civil society, because it advances the Organization's ideals, and helps support its work." www.unic-eg.org/eng/?page_id=318 (accessed 8-4-21).

Wikipedia defines it thus: "Civil society can be understood as the 'third sector' of society, distinct from government and business, and including the family and the private sphere. By other authors, civil society is used in the sense of 1) the aggregate of non-governmental organizations and institutions that manifest interests and will of citizens or 2) individuals and organizations in a society which are independent of the government." https://en.wikipedia.org/wiki/Civil_society (accessed 9-30-20). So that means that the self-designated Youth Climate Courts described in this book are civil society organizations.

1 How does a Youth Climate Court work?

> the child who is capable of forming his or her own views [has] the right
> to express those views freely in all matters affecting the child.
> International Convention on the Rights of the Child,
> Article 12, 1

Why conduct a Youth Climate Court?

The key value of Youth Climate Courts and the trials they organize and
conduct is that they provide a platform for young leaders to take action on
behalf of Earth and on behalf of their generation's and future generations'
well-being. Youth Climate Courts provide opportunity for young people
to speak truth to power and to effect real change in their communities.
Youth Courts thus provide young people both voice and agency, something so desperately needed in the face of the world-changing crisis they
and all of us are now facing.

Another important power Youth Climate Courts offer is the power to
remind communities and governments of the importance of respecting
human rights. One key fact about standards, after all, including human
rights standards, is that their power to persuade and compel is weakened
if they are not widely known, and is strengthened when they are publicly acknowledged, regularly appealed to, and exercised. So one function
of a Youth Climate Court will be to bring awareness of human rights
forward, to remind people about the rights due to them, and to remind
governments that they are obliged to protect and fulfill those rights for
their citizens.

This is one reason the world needs more human rights courts and why,
with so few of them yet in existence and with access so difficult, it will be
up to civil society organs, such as Youth Climate Courts, the Permanent
Peoples' Tribunal, and other similar institutions, to conduct human rights-
based court hearings publicly and regularly.

DOI: 10.4324/9781003217640-2

Whom should Youth Courts put on trial?

In a time when federal, provincial, and state governments are doing so little to address the climate crisis, and when those governments also feel so inaccessible to regular people, putting local city and county governments on trial seems the best place to start. After all, "Climate change is a global phenomenon, but it is people and communities at the local level that experience its consequences."[1] And equally important, movements such as Youth Climate Courts are most effective when those most affected, and those with the most moral authority on the issue, are engaged in urging the necessary changes.

Another reason to focus on local governments is because, as the battleship metaphor reminds us, it takes a long time and a huge energy expenditure to alter the course of a very large vessel. Changing the course of a small yacht or motor boat is less costly, though, and much less cumbersome. City governments, for example, are closer to home and city council members are more likely to have personal and friendly relationships with many people in town, including with people whom the Youth Court organizers know. Elected council members care about votes and care about how they are viewed by members of their immediate community. County boards of commissioners may also be good candidates to put on trial for similar reasons. Even local government agencies such as departments of transportation, or quasi-governmental agencies such as water districts and school boards, for example, could also be put on trial for failing to meet their human rights obligations with respect to climate change.

But why put governments, rather than private for-profit corporations, on trial? Corporations, after all, might be seen as the more obvious perpetrators when it comes to harming the Earth, oceans, atmosphere, climate and people. Some might say they cause harm in a more direct way than governments do. Governments, they could say, are only *allowing* the harm while corporations are directly *causing* it. Governments, it might be argued, only facilitate and enable harmful corporate behavior, but do not directly cause those harms themselves.

And yet there are important reasons why it would be less useful for Youth Climate Courts to put corporations on trial. Some of those reasons are similar to the reasons for not putting state and federal governments on trial: (1) they are just too large, (2) their leadership is far too distant and inaccessible, (3) their size and heft is too bulky and cumbersome and, like the battleship, less able to make major changes in short time frames, plus (4) large corporations, like large governments, are simply not as responsive to the wishes of ordinary citizens as local governments are likely to be, and (5) as private, for-profit entities they are much more obligated to the wishes of their owners/shareholders than they are to the wishes of ordinary citizens. Large corporations can thus more easily discount or ignore the wishes of ordinary citizens than can local governments.

Most important, though, for-profit corporations simply do not have the same kind of clear human rights obligations that governments have. For-profit corporations basically have one single mandate, which is to earn a profit and return it to their shareholders. That is their *raison d'être*. If they do not succeed at it, they go out of business and cease to exist. So their bottom line and primary focus has to be producing income. Any other actions that corporate leadership might consider undertaking will need to be weighed against that central purpose.

These are a few of the reasons why it will be more effective for Youth Climate Courts to focus their efforts on local governments rather than on large private, for-profit corporations. Governments, after all, do have clear human rights obligations, and local governments especially are close enough, accessible enough, and agile enough – certainly more agile than battleships – to seriously consider calls for major change.

Further, it is important that each level of government, commensurate with its scale, be committed to doing its part in the crisis. A recent ruling by a Dutch court, for example, required Royal Dutch Shell to do its share too by cutting its emissions dramatically by 2030. The court then added:

> "The court acknowledges that [Royal Dutch Shell] cannot solve this global problem on its own," the judgement reads. "However, this does not absolve RDS of its individual partial responsibility to do its part regarding the emissions of the Shell group, which it can control and influence."[2]

Similarly, even though a local government's contributions may seem small in comparison to the overall global need, taking responsibility for its full share of the work and its share of meeting human rights obligations will be essential. And if local governments shoulder their responsibility to work closely with other local governments, it will ultimately benefit everyone.

Roles of the Youth Climate Court team

And now we turn to specific details about how a Youth Climate Court trial can be organized and conducted. Let's begin with a review of the key functions and responsibilities of each person on the trial team.

The youth judge

The role of theYouth Climate Court judge is to formally open and preside over the trial, to indicate to the prosecuting and defense attorneys when it is their turn to make their case, to make sure everyone stays within their time limits, and to rule on any conflicts that might arise during the trial. The judge makes sure that the trial follows the Court's rules, ensures that witnesses promise to tell the truth when they are questioned and that no interrupting is allowed by either side or by attendees. For these functions the judge will need a gavel and a gentle, but clearly authoritative, manner.

After the prosecution and the defendant government have presented their closing arguments, the judge will instruct the young jury members as to what exactly the question is on which they will render a verdict,[3] where the jury room is in which their deliberations will take place, how much time they will have to discuss the issues and arrive at a verdict, and that they should take their deliberations very seriously. When the jury returns and hands the verdict to the judge, it will be the judge's job to ask the jury chairperson to stand and answer the judge's question as to what their verdict is.

The judge's response to the jury's decision will differ depending on whether the government is found guilty or not guilty. See "the verdict" section below.

Once the verdict has been rendered and the court's mandates have been issued (if the government is found guilty) then the trial is complete and the judge gavels the court session to a close.

The question to be decided

The question to which the court and jury will address themselves is this: given all that is required to address the climate crisis, has this government done an adequate job of doing its share to secure its citizens' rights with respect to the climate crisis? In other words, has this government adequately met its moral and legal obligation to protect and fulfill the human and constitutional rights[4] of its citizens with respect to mitigating and adapting to the climate crisis?

The prosecuting team will argue that the government has *not* adequately met its obligation to protect and fulfill the rights of its citizens with respect to the climate crisis. The elected official representing the government may argue that the government *has* adequately met that obligation, or at least has done its best and has made a good effort. The jury members, in their deliberations, will be deciding which argument best fits the facts.

The youth prosecuting team

The youth prosecuting attorney will be the person primarily responsible for organizing and presenting the case which argues that the defendant government has not been meeting its obligations to protect the rights of its community members,[5] especially of its youngest members and of upcoming generations. The youth prosecuting attorney will have one of the more demanding roles in the court proceedings. It would be to their benefit to have other team members assigned to help them with the preparatory research, organizing and preparing the argument, and finding and preparing witnesses. Prosecuting team members may even help the prosecuting attorney during the trial by calling and questioning witnesses and/or by delivering some portions of the argument.

The central theme of the prosecutor's argument[6] will be that the government's failures to act more aggressively are not taking the climate crisis seriously enough, that the government is not doing its part to address the crisis, is not living up to its primary obligations as a government, and is thus putting at serious risk the future and well-being of its people.

The prosecuting team may wish to call witnesses to help strengthen their case. These witnesses could testify to climate crisis impacts already being experienced – physical, biological, environmental, economic, psychological, familial, communal, and so on – and to even more serious effects to come. Witnesses may testify as to the government's primary responsibility, which is securing the rights of its citizens. Other witnesses may testify as to specific rights that are being put at risk by the crisis and the government's inaction. Because future generations will also be affected by the actions or inactions of governments today but literally have no voice to speak up for themselves, prosecutors may wish to call a witness who would speak for the interests of future generations. Witnesses could be young children or high school or college students, and could also be teachers, professors, experts, officials, authors of climate-related books or reports, or other respected or well-known public figures. Witnesses may testify in person (which would be ideal if the trial is conducted in person), or by phone, Facebook, Google, Zoom or other media platform.

Finding good witnesses to help support the case will require some initiative and creativity from the prosecutorial team. Sympathetic and articulate personal witnesses telling their own story can make a good case even stronger. Experts on specific aspects of the argument can also make a big difference. Most personal witnesses will probably live in or near the local community but expert witnesses could be drawn from anywhere in the world, limited only by the creativity of the prosecutorial team.

Organizers may also wish to invite *amicus curiae* briefs to be submitted ahead of the date set for the trial. *Amicus curiae*, or friend-of-the-court briefs, are simply statements submitted and entered into the court record by any other interested parties who would like to lend support to the prosecutor's case. *Amicus* briefs may be submitted by local, national or international NGOs (non-governmental organizations), by businesses, by religious organizations, by activists, or by any other public or private entity that sees itself as having an interest in the outcome of the trial. For examples of *amicus* briefs submitted to the Permanent Peoples' Tribunal Session on Human Rights, Fracking and Climate Change, see the Reports and *amicus* briefs page[7] of the PPT site.

Preparing the argument and practicing it well ahead of time will be essential, of course. Holding a dress-rehearsal mock session before the official trial takes place publicly could also help with identifying challenges and avoiding glitches. A dress-rehearsal would almost certainly help everyone feel more confident when it comes time for the actual public trial.

The youth liaison for the government representative to the court

After the Youth Court has issued its summons to the government and after the government has selected a representative to participate in the court's proceedings, it will help things run much more smoothly, and may even help a government feel more willing to participate and cooperate, if the Youth Climate Court organizing team assigns one of its members to be the friendly contact person assigned to help the government representative participating in the trial. The government representative will certainly have questions and if there is one person on the Youth Court team assigned to help them with answers and guidance, it may ease their minds and facilitate the whole process.

Youth jury members

The primary responsibility of jury members will be to listen carefully to the arguments presented in the courtroom by both sides, perhaps taking notes to help remember key points, then, when court arguments and witness testimony have been completed, to follow the judge's instructions and move to the private jury room (physical or online). The jurors will select a jury chairperson to lead and moderate the discussion. This could happen in the advance of the public trial or once the jury reaches the deliberation room. Once a chairperson has been selected, the jury's job will be to think carefully about the arguments, to discuss them candidly and respectfully, to take votes on the questions to be decided, and finally to decide what verdict they will render as a jury.

As noted above, the question the jury must answer is this: given all that will be required to address the climate crisis, has this government met its moral and legal obligation to protect and fulfill the rights of its citizens with respect to mitigating and adapting to the climate crisis?

The prosecuting attorney will have argued that the government did *not* do an adequate job. The defendant government may have argued that they *have* done an adequate job of protecting those rights. Or they may have argued instead that, despite their good will and best efforts, they just have not done an adequate job so far.

If jury members decide that the government has properly done its share of protecting and fulfilling the rights of its citizens with respect to the climate crisis, then it will render a verdict finding the government not guilty. If, on the other hand, jury members decide that the government has done an incomplete or inadequate job, they will render a verdict finding the government guilty as charged.

Once the decision has been made, the jury chairperson writes that simple verdict clearly on a piece of paper to later hand to the judge. Whether the jury decides to include any reasons for why they arrived at that verdict is entirely optional. The jury chairperson then sends a messenger to notify the judge that the jury has reached its verdict.

Media organizer (for news reporters, bloggers, social media outlets, etc.)

The more people who are made publicly aware of the trial, the more powerful its arguments and verdict will be and the more effective its mandates are likely to be. That means local newspapers, radio and TV stations, bloggers and other social media producers will all need to be kept informed about the trial and its developments. So there will need to be one person on the team whose entire role and responsibility is to organize publicity for the trial, making sure local media know about it ahead of time and keeping them updated throughout the lead-up to the trial, during the trial and throughout the trial's follow-up process as well.

Newspapers, TV, and radio outlets that make free Public Service Announcements may be able to announce the upcoming trial for no charge. Putting posters up in store windows on local bulletin boards, in libraries and in places where faith communities convene can help too.

Video-recording organizer

The team will probably want to live-stream the trial too, even if it is conducted in person, and will want to record it for others to view later. Having a video-archive of the trial will be useful to future Youth Climate Court organizers too so they can view it and learn from it. That means that whether the trial is conducted in person or online, it will be important to have someone on the team assigned to the job of organizing and conducting the live-streaming and recording of the trial so everyone else can focus on their own jobs without having to worry about whether all the technology is working.

Adult advisor or mentor?

The team may decide that it would benefit from having a teacher, professor, mentor, attorney, or other adult professional involved in the planning process to offer advice when needed, to help navigate certain practical details, and to help ease the path when the Youth Court team runs into snags. Snags are just part of the process and will almost certainly happen along the way. Each bump in the road, though, presents one more opportunity for the organizing team to engage its creativity and improvise ways to smooth out those bumps or navigate around them. Snags actually can, in the end, lead to fixes and revisions that result in making the whole trial even more effective than originally envisioned.

But will governments even show up?

Once summoned by a Youth Climate Court, will governments be inclined to step up, join in, and send a representative to the Court or not? If they have any good sense they certainly will, and even if some elected officials are only looking out for their own self-interest, they will also. Plus, most city and county governments these days include at least one or two members who, even if they are not in the majority, recognize the seriousness of the climate crisis and recognize that so little (or perhaps nothing) is being done locally to address it. Those members will want to show sympathy with the Youth Climate Court organizers and will want to participate in the trial if only out of respect for their young community members. Other elected members may just want to have their government's inaction be made public. Other members may welcome the Youth Climate Court's summons as a way of increasing public pressure for the government to do the right thing.

There is the old story about US President Franklin D. Roosevelt, after all, and the meeting he had with a group of activists who sought his support for some bold piece of legislation. He listened to their arguments for some time and finally said, "You've convinced me. Now go out and make me do it." Roosevelt understood that if people created more public pressure for his agenda, that would make it easier for him to actually implement it. Some local government officials may feel the same way about facing the climate crisis, hoping for increased public pressure to make them do what they already know needs to be done.

If, however, the government chooses to not participate, the Youth Court should proceed as planned and publicly call them out for that. If members of the government cared so little about the rights of its youth that they didn't even bother to respond, show up, and make their case, the public should know about that. "Perhaps," the media can be told, "they had no case to make. Perhaps they were ashamed of how little they had done."

And then the trial proceeds without them. A Youth Court defense attorney could possibly be assigned to represent the absent government if the organizing team so chooses, but that defense attorney could not be expected to make a very strong case, perhaps not any case at all, for a government that declined to even attend. Another option would be to simply include an empty chair somewhere in the Court's proceedings, as a representation of the government's failure to attend.

Most governments, though, will almost certainly decide to participate, even if only to avoid the moral stain of appearing to disrespect and disregard the passionately committed young people who are working so intently and so responsibly to protect the rights of everyone in their community.

Youth Climate Courts' teeth

Where exactly in this process are the Youth Court's teeth? What tools are available to the Youth Court to make sure the government respects its summons and shows up to the trial on the appointed day? And what can the Youth Court do to ensure that the government complies with the mandates it issues if the government is found guilty?

While Youth Climate Courts may not have the formal legal authority to compel change in the same way that a state or federal court does, what they do have is the moral authority of those whose lives are being directly impacted by the adult world's failure to act. And moral authority in situations like this can put pressure on those in power to comply. Young people today, in fact, living as they do under threat and pressure of a genuine life-changing climate emergency, are seen as clearly having more moral authority on this issue than do the many adult institutions that have done so little about the emergency, or who may even have ignored it almost completely.

If the Youth Climate Court chooses the restorative justice mandate (more on this later) to issue to the government, that too would help ensure that the government actually follows through on the changes it needs to undertake. Although the restorative justice approach is not exactly a form of "teeth," under the guidance of a trained restorative justice facilitator the process does normally lead to much more active buy-in from the participants. Both the Court and the government, in this case, would be actively engaged in listening respectfully to each other and determining together what specific actions will be required of the government and by what dates those actions must be completed.

Failing voluntary government engagement, though, Youth Courts do have the power to shame. Certainly, directing shame on others is no one's first choice. Nor is being publicly shamed by others. Most people would rather be publicly praised than publicly blamed. Sometimes, though, if nothing else seems to move a government and if an impending crisis is so pressingly imminent, so urgent and so threatening to so many people, then exercising the power to shame may need to be an option of last resort. And perhaps the power to shame is more exertable by young people on this issue today than at any time in the past. Governments do need to be called to account here, especially recalcitrant governments, for their inactions and failures. They do need to be made to listen, and who better to make them listen than those most directly wronged?

Engaging with local media is another kind of "teeth" and therefore a necessary ingredient in this process of exercising moral authority. This is why it will be so important for the Youth Court organizing team to have someone on board whose primary work is to inspire and ensure ongoing interest from local media.

The final set of "teeth," which no one wants to invoke, certainly, is the one affirmed in the second paragraph of the US *Declaration of Independence.* Among the truths that founders of the United States considered self-evident is the recognition that "whenever any Form of Government becomes destructive of these ends," that is, when any form of government fails to adequately protect the rights of its citizens,

> it is the Right of the People to alter or to abolish it, and to insti-
> tute new Government, laying its foundation on such principles and
> organizing its powers in such form, as to them shall seem most likely
> to effect their Safety and Happiness.[8]

The founders recognized that people do not want to change their government or even their government representatives "for light and transient causes." Most of us, says the *Declaration*, are actually "more disposed to suffer, while evils are sufferable" than to upend things to which we are accustomed. And yet ousting government officials, and sometimes whole governments, is certainly a time-honored response to major government failures.

What Youth Courts are ultimately calling for is an enormous change, a sea change really, in how things will be done in our climate-challenged world. Governments and communities may need to make significant changes in priorities and practices, and those changes are not likely to take place until communities are pressured to finally realize how desperately needed those changes are.

In this case a Youth Climate Court trial can be seen as akin to a family intervention in the life of an alcoholic or addict who has completely lost their way.[9] Youth Climate Court trials therefore, at least in the case of unresponsive or stubborn governments, are there to help force a government and community to realize that the human and ecological costs resulting from the climate crisis will be enormous. Their purpose, like that of an intervention, is to inspire the government to sit up, take notice, and do its part in making the serious changes necessary to protect the life and well-being of its community.

The prosecutor's argument

The prosecution's central argument will be relatively simple and straightforward. Its key elements will be to show (1) that respecting and realizing human rights is absolutely essential if people are to enjoy even a minimally decent life, (2) that it is government's central function and obligation to respect, protect, and fulfill those rights, (3) that the climate crisis puts at risk most or all human and constitutional rights, such as the rights to life, to security of person, to liberty, to water, to education, to health, to an adequate standard of living, to special care and assistance for women and children, and many other such rights, and (4) that this defendant government is failing in its fundamental moral obligation to do its share as a government to protect these rights. Each of those four elements in the basic argument will then need to be fleshed out in arguments, evidence, documents, and witnesses presented by the prosecution.

It may be useful, when the prosecution team is planning its argument, to consider using a technique prosecuting attorneys often use when beginning their oral arguments in a courtroom. They often open their argument with what they term a "roadmap," briefly laying out ahead of time each of the main points their argument will be making. They then can refer to that roadmap throughout their argument when they move on to their next point. This technique makes it easier for the judge and jury to follow the structure of the argument they are making.

The prosecutor(s) will want to draw particular attention to certain specific rights that they see as most clearly at risk in their climate-changed world. Chapter 3 of this book provides details about several of those specific rights prosecutors may decide to include in their arguments. A collection of the especially relevant declarations and covenants can be found on the Resources page[10] of the Youth Climate Courts website.

The verdict

Once the jury has completed its deliberations, voted, decided on its verdict and presented it to the judge, the judge then reads the verdict aloud to the Court and enters it as the first formal outcome of the trial. The second formal outcome will be the mandates the Court issues. Depending on what the verdict is, the judge announces the next step in the trial.

If not guilty

If the defendant government is acquitted because the youth jury has found it to be doing a strong and responsible job of protecting its citizens' rights, then the government is congratulated and urged to work with other local governments to encourage them to do more. At this point the Court's work with that government is completed.

If guilty

If the defendant government is found guilty of failing to adequately meet its human rights obligations, then the Court issues one or more formal mandates to that government requiring it to undertake certain specific actions, to complete them by a specific deadline, and to report back to the court as to the government's progress on those actions.

Issuing a mandate

Mandate options

Each Youth Court will need to determine which mandate(s) it considers most just and reasonable to issue to the government it has just found guilty. Several possibilities follow and Youth Court organizers may devise others.

Restorative justice process

Perhaps the most fruitful option, though somewhat more involved than the simpler and more direct options below, entails the Youth Court issuing a mandate requiring that the city or county enter into a formal restorative justice process with the Youth Court. This process allows the government and Court, together with the help of a trained restorative justice facilitator,[11] to schedule time together to listen carefully to each other's experience and perspective. Then together they explore and work out what the government needs to do to best meet its human rights obligations, to repair the harm being done especially to young people, and to restore a sense that just and effective responses to the climate crisis will be undertaken and will be ongoing.

The basic goal of the restorative justice process is for parties to hear and understand each other and then to work together to find just measures for repairing the harms caused by the actions or inactions of the guilty party. It is a cooperative process that allows those who have caused injury (by their action or inaction) and those who have suffered the injury to come together, listen attentively and respectfully to each other, acknowledge what has happened, and then to find an effective way to heal or ease the past injury and prevent future injuries. A well-done restorative justice process can lead to deep positive changes in individuals, in individual relationships, and in whole communities.

In the case of Youth Climate Courts, though, things are switched around a bit. In these climate cases, young people are the ones who have suffered and will suffer the injuries as a result of government failures. During the course of the trial, young people will have alleged that their government's failure to act has caused injury to them and will continue to cause further injury long into their future. So in this case the government is the perpetrator and young people are the victims. This approach, which locates the government in the position of offender, is true of virtually all human rights cases because in human rights cases governments are the duty-bearers, the ones with the obligation to protect their citizens' rights, and individuals are the rights-holders.

So if a Youth Climate Court finds a government guilty of failing to protect its citizens' rights, a restorative justice process will involve the perpetrator (government) and the injured parties (young people and their communities, represented by the Youth Court) coming together to listen to each other's experience and to work out what actions the government should take to remedy its past inaction. Required government actions that would result from this process could include the government first making a formal declaration of climate emergency and, second, developing a science-based, human rights-respecting Climate Action Plan, both to be completed by a certain date and submitted to the Youth Court for approval.

There are several advantages to a restorative justice approach. It allows the government that has just been found guilty to hear directly from young people about the depth of anxiety and grief they are feeling right now and the worry they experience when realizing what the climate crisis means for their future. It allows the government to recognize the fact of its inaction and to acknowledge that it has fallen down on the job. And also, because the process involves parties working together over time for a just outcome, it allows the Youth Court and government to develop a plan that can be more tailored to that particular government's situation and community circumstances. Perhaps most importantly, a restorative justice process enhances the commitment and sense of buy-in from both parties, and therefore increases the likelihood that the agreed-upon mandated plans will actually get completed and implemented by the government.[12] The restorative justice process also increases the probability that a satisfactory measure of justice will be actually be accomplished.

Climate emergency and Climate Action Plan

A somewhat simpler and more direct mandate the Court could issue would simply require the government to complete certain formal actions, such as declaring a climate emergency and/or developing a science-based and human rights-respecting[13] Climate Action Plan, both to be completed by a certain deadline and submitted back to the Youth Court for approval. The Youth Court then "retains jurisdiction" so that later, when the government has submitted its Climate Action Plan, the Court can reconvene, review the submitted plan and determine whether it does or does not meet the Court's standards of adequacy. If it does, the plan is returned as acceptable and the government is encouraged to monitor and publicly report on the implementation and efficacy of its plan.

Climate-in-all-policies rule

A third option would be for the Court to issue a mandate requiring that the government develop and enact a "climate-in-all-policies" rule for the city or county. Such a rule could read something like this:

> Before approval, every project proposed to be undertaken within the city (or county) must first undergo a climate impact review by the proposing government agency and/or by any related contractor. The review must be reported in writing to the city council (or county board of commissioners). Before the project is approved there must be a public hearing, announced in advance, with opportunity for citizen comment. The written report must include an unbiased summary of public comments and the report must be

expeditiously made available to the public. If approved, during project development the project must be monitored and evaluated for its climate impacts with the results reported in writing to the city council (or county board of commissioners) and the report made available to the public.[14]

Another version of this would be to require that the government develop a full science-based and human rights-respecting Climate Action Plan and include within it a "climate-in-all-policies" rule for the city or county.

Formally endorse and promote the Declaration on Human Rights and Climate Change

A fourth possible mandate would be to require the government to formally endorse, publicly display, and actively promote the Declaration on Human Rights and Climate Change. This means formally voting to endorse it, affixing council members' signatures to a poster-size copy[15] of the Declaration, displaying it prominently in a public area of the city or county office, and taking active measures to promote and underscore the Declaration's principles.[16]

Add climate language or amendment to founding document

Some nations, provinces, and states have begun to explicitly include environmental and climate goals directly in the government's founding constitutions or charters. New York state, for example, is currently considering an amendment to Article 1 of the state constitution which would read "Each person shall have a right to clean air and water and a healthful environment."[17] There is no reason that a city or county government could not consider adding something similar to its founding document as well. So a fifth possible mandate for a local government would be to require that the city or county review its charter to determine whether specific climate language should be included as revisions or amendments to its founding document.

Divest city or county investments from fossil fuel corporations

This mandate would require a government to immediately review its financial holdings to learn whether any of its funds are currently invested in fossil fuel corporations. If the review reveals that some of that government's holdings are invested in fossil fuel corporations, the government will immediately publicly disclose those investments and then make arrangements to divest and reinvest those funds in climate friendly companies.

Artistic installations

Other mandates might be somewhat less demanding for a government to take on and thus could be seen as ancillary to the primary mandates the Court issues. These could include requiring a local government to install a Climate Clock[18] to help make the community more aware of the urgency, or to require a local government to install a Climate Ribbon[19] in government buildings, libraries, or schools to give community members a chance to express "What they love and hope to never lose to climate chaos." Artistic installations like these may help underscore the crucial importance of the more directly applicable commitments the Youth Court is requiring of the government.

Any combination of the above

The Court could choose to mandate any one of, or any combination of, the above options, but included in whichever mandate(s) the Court even-tually issues will be the requirement to complete it by a given deadline. At the time the government's plan is submitted, if it does not meet the Court's standards of scientific and human rights adequacy, it will be formally returned (in person and in writing) to the government with instructions to improve it in certain ways or to develop a new, more satisfactory plan to be resubmitted to the Court by a given date. That process then continues until a submitted plan does meet the Court's standards of adequacy, at which point it is returned to the government with a request that the implementa-tion of its plan be closely monitored and publicly reported on.

Climate emergency declarations

A climate emergency declaration is simply a formal statement that puts a government on record as prioritizing action to do whatever it can to mitigate and adapt to the climate crisis. Such a declaration is a recogni-tion that the situation is dire, that the danger is imminent, and that dealing with it will require extraordinary measures. It means that the world is in the situation described by Winston Churchill on November 12, 1936, just prior to the outbreak of World War II.

"Owing to past neglect," he said, "in the face of the plainest warnings, we have entered upon a period of danger. The era of procrastination, of half measures, of soothing and baffling expedients of delays, is coming to its close. In its place we are entering a period of consequences ...We cannot avoid this period, we are in it now."[20]

According to the Climate Emergency Declaration website, 1,940 jurisdictions and local governments, covering 826 million citizens in 34 countries, have declared a climate emergency as of May 24, 2021.[21] There is no reason the local government on trial here should not consider declaring a climate emergency too. An emergency declaration, after all,

> shows that the government rates the problem as very serious, that priority will be given to resolving the crisis, that we are all in the crisis together and that, officially, with regard to the climate, 'business as usual' and 'reform as usual' no longer applies.[22]

For a more detailed understanding of what a climate emergency declaration entails for local governments, the Youth Court can refer local officials to the report, *Understanding climate emergency & local government.*[23]

A climate emergency declaration could be as simple as this one adopted by the City of Darebin, a few miles north of Melbourne in Australia:

> Council recognizes that we are in a state of climate emergency that requires urgent action by all levels of government, including by local councils.

The Darebin City Council has also produced a framework resource to help other city councils with their climate emergency response.[24] The Climate Mobilization website offers a fuller template for a climate emergency declaration as well.[25]

Milwaukie, Oregon in the United States was the first city in that state to declare a climate emergency (on January 21, 2020). The declaration is a straightforward, easily understandable, three-page document the central declaration of which reads

> Now be it therefore resolved, by the City Council of the City of Milwaukie, Oregon, that a climate and ecological emergency which threatens our city, region, state, nation, civilization, humanity and the natural world, is hereby declared;[26]

Local school boards and universities can also declare a climate emergency. On September 20, 2019, for example, the University of Warwick, in England, made this following formal declaration of a climate emergency:

Recognising that the next ten years will be crucial to limit global temperature rise the University of Warwick is now declaring a state of Climate Emergency.

We have a responsibility as a community and organisation to help combat climate change through our individual actions, our research and teaching, and how we run and develop our university.

However declaring a climate emergency must be matched with ambitious plans and goals so the University is announcing that it aims to reach net zero carbon from our direct emissions and the energy we buy by 2030.

We will also work with our community to put in place initiatives to significantly reduce our indirect emissions with the aim of achieving net zero carbon for both direct and indirect emissions by 2050.[27]

In another example, the University of Sydney (Australia) Law School voted unanimously on December 6, 2019 to declare a climate emergency based on the 2018 finding of the Intergovernmental Panel on Climate Change that to avoid a more than 1.5°C rise in global warming, global emissions need to fall by around 45 percent from 2010 levels by 2030, reaching net zero by around 2050. Their declaration was inspired by "the clear and unequivocal declaration of 11,000 climate scientists on November 5, 2019[28] that they have a moral obligation to advise that planet Earth is facing a climate emergency."[29]

These last two examples are university declarations rather than government declarations, but they can still provide guidelines for other universities, for local school boards and even for local governments as they draft their own emergency declarations.

Declarations must be followed by actual climate-protection actions, of course, which is why the mandate from a Youth Climate Court should require both the emergency declaration and formal government action such as the development of a Climate Action Plan.

Climate Action Plans

Climate Action Plans (CAPs) can vary significantly from one city or county government to another depending on the physical size, population size, geographical location of its jurisdiction, and demographic make-up of its citizenry. There are many examples of Climate Action Plans available on the web that can be downloaded and modified to fit a government's and community's particular situation. It is essential, though, that all Climate Action Plans be solidly based in science and explicitly committed to respecting and securing human rights in all climate-related mitigation and adaptation measures, including those specific rights outlined in Chapter 3.

1   When it comes to climate *mitigation,* city councils, county boards of commissioners, agency directors, school boards, etc. will want to make sure that their Climate Action Plan includes commitments to significant reductions in reliance on fossil fuels and to reduction of CO_2 and methane emissions over the coming years. This can be accomplished by making improvements to public transport and to safe walking and bicycling options, by incentivizing a switch to electric vehicles, by supporting more rooftop and community solar and other renewable energy development projects, by supporting a move to smaller and better weatherized homes, electric power in all new construction, minimizing waste production, and so on.

2   Governments will also want to make sure their Climate Action Plan includes support for measures, public and private, that foster carbon sequestration in forests, vegetation and soils, including support for regenerative agriculture practices and support for urban and rural preservation and planting of trees.

3   On the climate *adaptation* side, it is becoming increasingly clear, from experience in various parts of the world already impacted by climate-related disasters, that disasters will present new kinds of challenges in a climate-changed world. Natural disasters in the past have often come as single events that arrived, passed, and then allowed communities some time to recover. In a climate-changed world, however, such disasters will become increasingly repetitive, intense, interconnected and cumulative. Such intensified disaster experience scenarios dramatically raise the risk of increased Post-traumatic Stress Disorder, anxiety, depression, disabling grief, and similar mental health challenges in communities. Those challenges can sometimes lead to increases in drug and alcohol addiction, aggression, spousal and child abuse, and so on. All these challenges can be even more pronounced in under-resourced and historically marginalized communities. So Climate Action Plans will want to include measures for addressing those added consequences in their disaster planning as well.

4   Finally, The United Nations *Safe Climate* report[30] prepared by the UN Special Rapporteur on Human Rights and the Environment includes a collection of specific actions that local governments can implement and/or include in their Climate Action Plans. Those actions can, for example, include protection of the specific rights detailed in Chapter 3. Climate Action Plans must also ensure respect

for the rights of the child, the rights of Indigenous peoples and the rights of other vulnerable populations.

A list of measures that local governments should consider including in their Climate Action Plans can be found in Appendix IV.

A community climate advisory and accountability board could be created with responsibility to flesh out the CAP and to make sure it includes specific actionable measures with specific deadlines. The board's responsibilities would also include making clear who will be accountable for completing which parts of the CAP and by which deadlines. It will also want to make sure the CAP includes plans for monitoring progress through time and updating the plan as necessary. Adequate budgeting and staffing will be essential as well.

Further, Youth Climate Court organizers need to ensure that the government follows through on its mandates. This may require the Youth Court to keep pressure on that government to insure that it meets its court-imposed deadlines. This could mean that Youth Court organizers and officers (i.e., the youth judge, prosecutors and jury members) would (1) physically attend city or county council meetings, (2) arrange interviews with local media, (3) hold public demonstrations, (4) collaborate with other interested groups or individuals to apply pressure, (5) bring national or international pressures to bear on the local government, and so on. This need to keep the pressure on will call for creative new measures to inspire governments to act or, if necessary, new ways to threaten shame.

Finally, when issuing its mandates, the Youth Court may wish to appeal to the concept of "the good ancestor" and remind council members that when future generations look back on these times, elected officials will want to be seen by their grandchildren and great-grandchildren as "good ancestors" whose decisions and actions showed foresight, wisdom, and care for their future offspring's well-being for generations to come.

International coalition of Youth Courts

As more Youth Climate Court trials are conducted around the world, the International Coalition of Youth Courts[31] will become an increasingly useful resource to offer help with trainings for Youth Climate Court organizing teams. Teams that have completed their trials can offer to future teams best-practices suggestions for organizing, preparing for, and conducting court sessions. The ICYC will also serve as a research center for studying the procedures, verdicts, mandates, effectiveness, and long-term impacts of Youth Climate Courts around the world.

If even a few of these Youth Courts are developed and conducted around the world, they could potentially, with such strong youth voices, bring about real change in the policies, practices, and mindset of the governments they put on trial.

If *more* than a few such courts are conducted, though, the effects could become globally significant, a kind of "youthquake," a rumbling from below that shakes the adult world from the ground up, effecting real change through the people-power of local governments.

As each court trial reports its results, ideas, and suggestions to the International Coalition of Youth Courts, organizers of future Youth Courts will be able to learn from the experience of those who have gone before. In this way the Coalition can serve several purposes. It can:

- collect suggestions for how to approach and work with a defendant government;
- offer suggestions for engaging with local media to maximize publicity;
- collect ideas and materials for building strong prosecutorial arguments;
- help identify which kinds of arguments have proven most effective in past trials, and how best to present them;
- help identify which kinds of evidence have been most effective in arguments, and where to find that evidence;
- help identify which kinds of witnesses have been most persuasive and effective, and how best to locate them, prepare them, and elicit their testimony during the trial;
- help organizers understand human rights, what they mean, how they work, and how best to use them in a trial;
- help identify best practices for setting up and conducting a court session;
- help identify available restorative justice resources and facilitators for teams whose mandate requires the restorative justice process;
- it could, with time and experience, eventually serve as a training center to help with organizing future Youth Courts, perhaps even being available as a resource during the process of conducting a trial.

As a center supporting research on Youth Courts, the Coalition will:

- serve as an archive for recordings, supporting documents, and miscellaneous planning notes from Youth Climate Court trials that have already taken place;
- serve as an archive for the trial verdicts, mandates issued to governments, and compliance records of governments that have been put on trial;

- keep records of how defendant governments have responded to their summons, how they have behaved during the court hearings, and how well they have carried out the mandates that resulted from their court sessions;
- serve as a records repository for future researchers interested in human rights, climate change and the effectiveness of Youth Climate Courts as civil society change-makers.

The International Coalition can thus, over time, serve all these purposes and can also document what the experience has been like for the young people who have organized and conducted these trials.

Basic steps in the process of developing a Youth Climate Court

A simple listing of basic steps involved in putting together a Youth Climate Court trial may be helpful as a starting place for teams when they first start thinking about how to plan a trial. So a preliminary list of steps is offered here for use and liberal modification by individual teams.

1   Gather interested team members who will volunteer to be on the YCC team. Members then democratically decide who will serve specific roles. A complete list of roles can be found earlier in Chapter 1.
2   Decide which local government, government agency or department to put on trial for failing to adequately protect the community's human rights. Possible government bodies could include the city or county government; the school board; a planning commission; the department of transportation, forestry, or agriculture, etc.
3   Decide whether any adults (mentors, teachers, professors, community members, parents, etc.) will be asked to help throughout the process, determine the extent of their involvement and decide how you would like them to help.
4   Decide whether the trial will be conducted in person or online, the trial date and – if it will be conducted in person – the best location for the trial.
5   Decide on the approximate length of time for conducting the trial (two hours? half a day? a full day?) and how much time will be allotted for each portion – prosecutor's and defendants' cases, witness testimony and questioning of witnesses, closing arguments by each side, jury deliberations, announcement of the verdict, issuing of the mandates, etc.
6   Write a short one-page description of what this Youth Climate Court is and what the trial will entail. This will be the document

that is handed to anyone interested in the trial, to the media, and especially to members of the government that will be put on trial. Then write an even shorter one paragraph, elevator-speech version too. This will be useful later whenever, for example, someone asks what you've been doing lately.

7   The person assigned to public media should connect with as many local media and social media leaders as possible and invite them to cover the trial. The more media coverage, the more influence the Court will have.

8   Youth Court officers (judge, attorneys, jury members) begin preparing for their roles, formulating their arguments, locating witnesses, etc., and planning details as to exactly how the trial will proceed.

9   Locate a dignified, court-like venue for conducting the trial; or, if the trial will be conducted online, identify which technologies and locations will be used.

10 Because the Court's outcome may result in requiring the defendant government to prepare a science-based, human rights-respecting Climate Action Plan, this will be the time to think through what the Court will consider adequate for such a plan, or adequate at least for the government's process for developing such a plan.

11 While Youth Court officers are preparing their arguments and roles, now will be the time to contact members of the defendant government and explain that there will be a trial, that it will be conducted publicly and covered by media. Formally invite the government, in person and in writing, to send to the trial a representative who can explain the government's point of view and defend its interests.

12 Consider conducting a dress-rehearsal, mock court session prior to the public court session to practice and work out any glitches.

13 On the appointed day, everyone takes their places and the judge formally calls the Court to order.

   a   The youth judge presides over the proceedings. The prosecutor(s) submit any material they have prepared, present their arguments, call and question witnesses. The defendants do the same.

   b   When the prosecution and defense have completed their closing arguments, the youth jury retires to the deliberation room. There, they discuss, vote, and decide on a verdict.

   c   The jury returns to the Court and the chairperson reads the verdict. If the defendant government is found not guilty, the Court congratulates the government and encourages them to work with other governments to address the climate crisis. If the defendant government is found guilty, then the Court issues one or more formal mandates to the government.

d   Before the trial concludes, the judge announces that the Youth
Court will "retain jurisdiction" until the mandate's requirements
have been met.

e   The judge thanks all participants and gavels the proceedings to
a close.

This Youth Climate Courts model offers some big advantages both to
young activists and to the governments they will be addressing.

1   Youth Climate Courts provide young people direct access to real
governments and their elected officials, direct access in the process
of issuing a summons, direct access during the lead-up to the trial,
direct access during the trial itself, and direct access during the trial's
follow-up when Youth Court organizers are monitoring whether the
government is following through on its mandates.

2   Youth Climate Courts give young people a way to directly exert
genuine, up-close-and-personal pressure on their local governments.

3   Youth Climate Courts call on those governments to think in much
bigger terms than they ever have to date, and to consider some of the
more demanding measures that will be necessary for dealing with the
climate crisis.

4   There is scant evidence so far that adults have, on their own, been able
to take on the large and politically difficult policy proposals necessitated
by the climate crisis without direct pressure from young people in
their community, young people whom they know personally and care
about. The deep moral urgency of direct appeals from young people
can actually make it easier for governments to undertake the kind of
major policy initiatives that they know will be necessary.

5   Finally, while it will of course be important for the organizing team
to take its work seriously and make the court session as dignified,
professional and meaningful as possible, still, the time, energy and
teamwork that goes into planning a court session like this will also
be exciting and rich with learning, camaraderie, and the making of
good friendships. Enjoyable work with good friends helps insure
that the project will be done creatively, efficaciously and with
passion and heart. The courtroom itself will be a time of gravitas
and decorum, of course, befitting such a crucially important task,
but the hard work of preparation can also be enjoyable and deeply
gratifying.

6   Team members can also know that their good work will be extremely
useful to future organizing teams who will learn from the experiences
of those who have come before them. They can know, too, that their
good work, along with the results and outcomes of their Youth

Climate Court trial, will help garner crucial public support for larger, formal court cases brought in state and federal courts, such as *Juliana v. the United States, La Rose v. Her Majesty the Queen in Canada*, and the many other rights-based climate cases being brought in state, national, and international courts around the world.

Adaptable, flexible, malleable, innovative

These steps offer a model for how organizing a Youth Climate Court can be done. There is plenty of room, though, for creativity and innovation at each stage of the planning process. Considerations about the specific local government and its situation and make-up, along with the thoughtful, wise judgments of the organizing team and their mentors, may lead to modifications about which government entity to put on trial, how best to garner publicity, what the outline and scope of the prosecutorial argument should be, and so on. In other words, these steps above offer a general template for organizing a Youth Climate Court trial. They show one vision of what a strong Youth Climate Court trial looks like. But these courts are also adaptable, flexible, and open to creative forms of implementation depending on the local situation and on the good judgment of the organizing team and its mentors.

Here is just one example of possible variations.

These Youth Climate Courts, as we have seen, are grounded in human rights standards as expressed in international human rights covenants, declarations and treaties. This is so for all the reasons laid out above and explained more fully in Chapter 2. These human rights covenants and declarations can be viewed as statements of moral standards (grounded in law) or as strictly legal standards (based on moral norms). So if we imagine a spectrum that, on one end, views human rights as primarily *moral* standards and on the other end views human rights as primarily *legal* standards, different variations in how Youth Climate Courts are conducted can fall anywhere along that spectrum, depending on the interests and legal expertise of a Youth Court's organizers.

The paradigmatic Youth Climate Court model described in this book, though, clearly leans more toward the "human rights as moral standards" end of that spectrum, partly to underscore how deeply moral the climate crisis is and partly to make sure these Youth Courts are accessible to more young people around the world, many of whom will not be familiar with the intricacies of statutory and common law practice. And partly, too, because human rights as moral standards may resonate more both with the local elected officials who are being called to account and with their local communities.

Doubtless, though, there will be variations on this Youth Climate Courts model that lean more toward the "human rights as legal standards" end of the spectrum, especially when the organizers are law students or others who are familiar with the intricacies of legal practice. But to keep the Youth Court model as widely accessible as possible, and accessible to as wide an age-range and schooling-range as possible, the paradigmatic Youth Climate Court case will lean more toward the "human rights as moral standards" end of the spectrum and will provide a platform for the passionate moral urgency that so many young people feel today.

Notes

1 Oregon Public Broadcasting, *Oregon Call to Action on Climate, Health and Equity.* 2-5-20. www.oregonpublichealth.org/assets/Oregon%20CALL%20 TO%20ACTION.pdf (accessed 2-15-20).
2 Antonia Juhasz, "A Court Ruled Shell Is Liable for Its Contributions to Climate Change. What Happens Now?" *Rolling Stone*, 5-27-21. www.rollingstone.com/politics/politics-features/shell-climate-change-oil-dutch-court-1175404/ (accessed 5-27-21).
3 See next section, "The question to be decided."
4 If the organizing team decides to include constitutional rights in their case.
5 See the specific human rights section in Chapter 3 of this book.
6 See "the prosecutorial argument" section below.
7 www.tribunalonfracking.org/submitted-testimony/.
8 www.archives.gov/founding-docs/declaration-transcript.
9 See the Coda at the end of this book.
10 www.youthclimatecourts.org/resources-for-ycc-planning/.
11 For help locating trained Restorative Justice facilitators, contact the Zehr Institute for Restorative Justice. https://zehr-institute.org.
12 The National Conflict Resolution Center is a valuable online resource for RJ practice. www.ncrconline.com. Howard Zehr is regarded as "the grandfather of restorative justice" and his classic book, *The Little Book of Restorative Justice*, is very helpful. www.amazon.com/Little-Book-Restorative-Justice-Peacebuilding/dp/1561488232/ref=sr_1_3?dchild=1&keywords=zehr&qid=16040 99319&sr=8-3.
13 The human-rights respecting Climate Action Plan should include a listing of key applicable human and constitutional rights. "The provision of rights in law has little meaning if citizens are unaware of them or cannot exercise them. Governments should publicize the rights available to the public and ensure a robust, free civil society able to help citizens actuate these rights." – *Environmental Rule of Law, First Global Report*, 2019, Section 4, "Rights," p. 182.

14 Sample wording suggested in private correspondence by Dr Bill Wiist, Courtesy Faculty, Global Health Program, College of Public Health and Human Sciences, Oregon State University.

15 A poster-size version of the Declaration on Human Rights and Climate Change is available on the Resources page of the Youth Climate Courts website. www.tribunalonfracking.org/wp-content/uploads/2019/03/DHRCC-poster-size-1.pdf.

16 For further information about the genesis, intent and provisions of the Declaration on Human Rights and Climate Change, see Kirsten Davies et al., '"The Declaration on Human Rights and Climate Change': A New Legal Tool for Global Policy Change," *Journal of Human Rights and the Environment* 8(2) September 2017.

17 www.nny360.com/news/government/new-york-environmental-rights-headed-for-public-vote-this-year/article_f7bf1dde-bcd0-5171-83cc-3b6f0b29ebcf.html.

18 https://climateclock.world.

19 www.theclimateribbon.org.

20 Paul Gilding, *Climate Emergency Defined: What is a Climate Emergency and Does the Evidence Justify One?* Breakthrough - National Centre for Climate Restoration, Melbourne, Australia. September 2019. https://52a87f3e-7945-4bb1-abbf-9aa66cd4e93e.filesusr.com/ugd/148cb0_3be3bfab3f3a489cb9bd69e42ce22e7c.pdf (accessed 22-7-21).

21 The jurisdictions and in which countries they are located are listed here: https://climateemergencydeclaration.org/climate-emergency-declarations-cover-15-million-citizens/ (accessed 5-30-21).

22 www.emeraldology.com/tacoma-joined-hundreds-of-cities-in-declaring-climate-emergency-what-does-it-mean-and-should-seattle-follow-suit/

23 www.breakthroughonline.org.au/guides (accessed 1-13-21).

24 *Framework for Effective Local Government Climate Emergency Response.* https://drive.google.com/file/d/0B1_MgvZlGIyVdkI3YktEWlVQV3laN05oTkp Cd0FxTVVocEVV/view (accessed 1-22-20).

25 www.theclimatemobilization.org/climate-emergency-resolution (accessed 1-22-20).

26 www.milwaukieoregon.gov/sites/default/files/fileattachments/sustainability/page/111121/r7-2020.pdf (accessed 17-8-21).

27 https://warwick.ac.uk/newsandevents/pressreleases/university_of_warwick_climate_emergency_declaration1/ (accessed 8-5-21).

28 There are currently 13,766 signatories from 156 countries as of 11-2-20. https://scientistswarning.forestry.oregonstate.edu.

29 "That The University of Sydney Law School declares a climate emergency following the finding of the Intergovernmental Panel on Climate Change in 2018 that to avoid a more than 1.5°C rise in global warming, global emissions need to fall by around 45 per cent from 2010 levels by 2030, reaching net zero by around 2050;

Acknowledging that global temperatures have already warmed by 1°C and heeding the clear and unequivocal declaration of 11,000 climate scientists on 5 November 2019 that they have a moral obligation to advise that planet Earth is facing a climate emergency;

Heeding the further warning of climate scientists, dated 28 November 2019, that 'tipping points' in the Earth's climate system may be reached between 1-2°C of warming;

Recognising the devastating environmental, social and economic impacts that climate change, including extreme weather events, is having, and will continue to have in Australia and globally;

Recognising that the United Nations Environment Program's Emissions Gap Report, dated 29 November 2019, states that countries' efforts under the Paris Agreement must increase fivefold to avoid a more than 1.5°C rise in global warming and threefold to avoid a more than 2°C rise;

Recognising the World Meteorological Organization's finding of 3 December 2019 that concentrations of carbon dioxide in the atmosphere hit a record level of 407.8 parts per million in 2018 and continued to rise in 2019;

Recognising that as legal academics we have a moral duty to stand up, speak out and express our concern, from a justice perspective, for all of the people, ecosystems and species across the world facing an existential threat;

Affirming that addressing and adapting to the climate emergency is critical to The University of Sydney Law School's core functions of research, teaching and community engagement;

Recognising the indispensable role of law and legal institutions in Australia and globally in implementing the Paris Agreement and achieving its objectives;

Emphasising the vital contribution that law teachers and researchers will need to make in developing effective and just responses to the climate emergency;

Committing ourselves to educating students about the climate emergency and legal responses to it;

Supporting the development of The University of Sydney's Sustainability Strategy, and efforts to achieve carbon neutrality across the University's operations.

Consequently, The University of Sydney Law School calls on the Australian government, and all governments around the world, to scale up their emissions reduction commitments made under the Paris Agreement consistently with the science, implement these commitments in comprehensive climate legislation covering all emissions and sectors, and prepare their countries for the climate emergency.

All governments and non-governmental entities around the world, including corporations, are called on, in line with the Paris Agreement, to:

(a) rapidly phase out the use of fossil fuels and transition to a clean energy system;
(b) safeguard the dignity, wellbeing and economic future of workers and communities in carbon intensive sectors; and

(c) move swiftly to capture the economic opportunities and green jobs in a low carbon economy." https://sydney.edu.au/law/news-and-events/news/2019/12/11/university-of-sydney-law-school-climate-emergency-declaration.html.

30 www.ohchr.org/Documents/Issues/Environment/SREnvironment/Report.pdf.
31 /www.youthclimatecourts.org/introduction/.

2 What are human rights?

Because the trials in Youth Climate Courts are built around human rights standards and because local governments will be put on trial for failing to protect the human rights of people in their communities, especially of their children, Youth Climate Court teams will want to have a good understanding of what human rights are, where they come from, how they apply to governments, and even a little something about their modern history. Chapter 2 offers a brief overview of just those aspects of human rights.

But first, to begin, a few words about exactly how rights are being threatened and undermined by the climate crisis. We have known for at least a decade that the climate crisis puts human rights standards at severe risk. Back in 2010, for example, it was known even then that, "as a matter of simple observation,

> climate change will undermine – indeed, is already undermining – the realisation of a broad range of internationally protected human rights: rights to health and even life; rights to food, water, shelter and property; rights associated with livelihood and culture; with migration and resettlement; and with personal security in the event of conflict. Few dispute that this is the case."[1]

Then in 2015, two United Nations reports were issued detailing just how the climate crisis threatens the realization and fulfillment of human rights. One report was issued by the United Nations Environment Programme (UNEP)[2] and the other by the Office of the United Nations High Commissioner for Human Rights (UNHCHR).[3]

More recently, in the 2019 United Nations *Safe Climate* report, Dr David Boyd, the UN Special Rapporteur on Human Rights and the Environment, wrote that climate change is already having "a major impact

DOI: 10.4324/9781003217640-3

on a wide range of human rights today, and could have a cataclysmic impact in the future unless ambitious actions are undertaken immediately. Among the human rights being threatened and violated," he continues,

> are the rights to life, health, food, water and sanitation, a healthy environment, an adequate standard of living, housing, property, self-determination, development and culture. Addressing climate change raises issues of justice and equity, both between and within nations and generations. The main contributors to the problem have reaped immense economic benefits and thus have the greatest responsibility to solve the problem … The adverse impacts of climate change disproportionately affect people living in poverty, whose contribution to the problem is minimal and who lack the resources to protect themselves or to adapt to the changes.[4]

Chapter 3 will provide more detail about several of those specific rights – to life, health, food, water, and others. At this point, though, it is worth underscoring, as does the 2015 Paris Climate Agreement, signed in 2016 by all Earth's 195 nations,[5] that when governments begin to take action against climate change they should

> promote and consider their respective obligations on human rights, the right to health, the rights of indigenous peoples, local communities, migrants, children, persons with disabilities and people in vulnerable situations and the right to development, as well as gender equality, empowerment of women and intergenerational equity.[6]

Because respecting and fulfilling human rights is morally obligatory for governments, and because human rights are the foundation and moral center of Youth Climate Court cases, it will be important to understand what role they will play in prosecutors' arguments, and what kinds of moral and sometimes legal power they bring to discussions about the climate crisis. Chapter 2 is intended to help with those questions and Chapter 3 offers more detail about some specific rights that are directly impacted by the climate crisis.

What are human rights?

Human rights standards are justified moral claims universally held by all persons vis-à-vis their governments, allowing them the opportunity to enjoy, at the very least, the bare minimums of a decent life. As constitutional scholar Ronald Dworkin puts it:

> To have a right to x is to be entitled to x. it is owed to you, belongs to you in particular. And if x is threatened or denied, right-holders are authorized to make special claims that ordinarily trump utility, social policy, and other moral or political grounds for action.[7]

Further, basic human rights are not just lofty aspirational ideals. Most, rather, are moral floors, moral minimums, delineating the most basic requirements for a person to live a minimally decent life. Failure to respect these minimal norms offends the conscience and often provokes moral outrage. The Preamble of the Universal Declaration of Human Rights (UDHR), for example, reminds us, right at the beginning, that neglecting human rights can provoke justifiable outrage: "disregard and contempt for human rights have resulted in barbarous acts which have outraged the conscience of mankind."[8] One of the drafters of the UDHR, Carrare Andrade from Ecuador, spoke for many of his colleagues when he said that the declaration "was the most important document of the century, and indeed ... a major expression of the human conscience."[9]

So, just as civil laws represent hard *legal* boundaries outside of which certain behaviors are not legally permissible, human rights standards represent hard *ethical* boundaries outside of which certain behaviors are not morally permissible. This means that when a government is being held accountable for failing to respect its human rights obligations, that government is actually being held to only the very lowest standard of moral acceptability.

Modern history of human rights

A quick overview of when and how the modern human rights movement began will start with the 1948 Universal Declaration of Human Rights, developed right after World War II in response to those "barbarous acts which have outraged the conscience of mankind."[10] The barbarous acts referred to, in the 1930s and 1940s in Germany's Third Reich, were undertaken in a modern, educated, cultured, western democracy, in full compliance with democratically enacted laws, all regulated and overseen by administratively legitimate government ministries, and legally carried out by government workers in those ministries. And yet were brazenly destructive of human life, well-being, and dignity.

We can all see now, of course, that those actions were wrong and deeply horrendous despite being entirely legal in Germany's legal system at the time. And yet there was no clear notion at the time, no publicly validated framework for thinking about how some laws, some legally enacted statutes and policies, could be considered unjust and immoral.

Then came the UDHR in 1948, a unique, brand-new thing in the world. Human rights scholar Jonathan Morsink explains what was so momentous about this event. "In the world of ethics," he says,

> something genuinely unique came into the world with the signing and adoption of the UDHR. Never before in human history had a document about moral values been conceived, written, and endorsed by representatives of virtually every nation on earth. René Cassin, one of the drafters of the UDHR (who, for his work, was awarded the Nobel Peace Prize in 1968), is quoted as saying that, with the UDHR, "something new ... entered the world." It was, he said, "the first document about moral value adopted by an assembly of the human community."[11]

This was a truly remarkable development.

The UDHR is a statement about the rights that are justly due to every human being on earth. Unfortunately, not everyone is aware of the rights which are due to them and which governments are obliged to respect. "[C]itizens may be unaware of their rights under human rights treaties as well as under national constitutions and laws ... [and therefore] unaware of the recourse they might have."[12] Aware or not, though, citizens do have these rights and are authorized to make claims on governments to ensure that those rights are respected.

Though the UDHR was framed as a declaration only, not as an actionable, operational treaty in international law, two legally binding international covenants did subsequently follow adoption of the UDHR – the International Covenant on Civil and Political Rights[13] (ICCPR) and the International Covenant on Economic, Social and Cultural Rights[14] (ICESCR). Those human rights treaties are binding law in the countries that have signed and ratified them. Those three documents together (the UDHR, the ICCPR, and the ICESCR) are now recognized as constituting the International Bill of Rights.

Human rights as moral and legal standards

Human rights are thus recognized as both moral imperatives to guide the behavior of governments and as legally binding law. Human rights standards are considered binding law in the narrowest legal sense only in those countries which have signed and ratified the international covenants and conventions in which those rights are delineated. In a broader sense, though, they are considered binding law to the extent that they have become "customary law" throughout the broader international community.[15]

Far more importantly, though, as *moral* imperatives these rights lay down the most basic elements of what is considered necessary for people to live a minimally decent life. These elements include the rights to life, to health, to food, to water, and to an environment capable of sustaining human life. Human rights norms thus lay down the lowest minimum standards for acceptable government behavior.

Mary Robinson, the former president of Ireland (1990-1997), the former UNHCHR (1997-2002), and founder of the Mary Robinson Foundation Climate Justice, says it clearly: "The idea of human rights points societies toward internationally agreed values around which common action can be negotiated and then acted upon." She continues,

> Human rights yardsticks deliver valuable minimal thresholds, legally defined, about which there is widespread consensus. The guarantee of basic rights rooted in respect for the dignity of the person which is at the core of this approach makes [human rights] an indispensable foundation for action on climate justice.[16]

Why human rights?

Human rights are recognized as basic moral minimums for governments to respect and fulfill because, as we have mentioned above and will see more fully below, the primary function of a government is to secure the rights of its citizens. The climate crisis, though, threatens to undermine the fulfillment of many, perhaps all, human rights. So human rights norms serve as the clear moral standard against which a government's climate policies and practices must be measured. They are also the ideal standard, both moral and legal, for Youth Climate Courts to use when calling their local government to account.

For one thing human rights norms set clear standards, minimum standards, for what duty-bearing governments must do, and standards too for what governments must avoid doing. These standards, which apply universally to governments around the world as well as to subnational governments within each nation, draw a clear line between behaviors that are considered morally acceptable and those condemned as morally reprehensible.

Another reason that Youth Climate Courts are grounded in human rights standards is because human rights are universal, not parochial. They are not limited to certain peoples, groups, religions, nations, or situations. Rather, human rights are universal in at least these following three senses.

First, they are universal in the sense that they arose out of a broad human consensus across the world. As human rights scholar Johannes Morsink reminded us above, the 1948 adoption of the UDHR was the first time in human history that representatives of virtually every nation on earth came together and officially adopted a formal statement of moral values.

Second, human rights are promulgated universally. The UDHR is, for example, the most widely translated document in the world. To date, it has been translated into over 500 languages, including at least two sign languages.[17]

Third, human rights standards formally apply to all persons everywhere, including children, because of the simple fact that they are human persons. According to the United Nations High Commission for Human Rights:

> Human rights are rights we have simply because we exist as human beings - they are not granted by any state. These universal rights are **inherent** to us all, regardless of nationality, sex, national or ethnic origin, color, religion, language, or any other status. They range from the most fundamental - the right to life - to those that make life worth living, such as the rights to food, education, work, health, and liberty.[18]

This is why it can be said that human rights – at least, those articulated in and implied by the UDHR - are the closest thing the world has ever had to a globally agreed upon set of moral standards.

Another advantage of using human rights standards is that they are recognized as taking precedence over other, potentially conflicting, considerations in government policy-making such as utility, cost-benefit analysis, economic value and social value. As human rights scholar Jack Donnelly puts it, "rights are *prima facie* trumps."[19] And as American legal philosopher and constitutional scholar Ronald Dworkin says, "individual rights are political trumps held by individuals." This means that rights claims take precedence over other considerations when issues of rights are at stake.[20] The institution of rights, says Dworkin, "represents the majority's promise to the minorities that their dignity and equality will be respected,"[21] and, therefore, that rights must be given the greatest weight in policy-making decisions.

Yet another major benefit of the human rights framework is that it views behaviors and responsibilities less from the perspective of the powerful, the moneyed, and the privileged and more from the viewpoint of the poor, the disenfranchised, the unempowered, the non-privileged, the injured, the marginalized, workers, Indigenous peoples, women, and children. It also weighs judgments through the eyes of future generations who are, in this context, literally voiceless, unable to speak up for their own interests. And these particular people and groups are precisely the ones most power-fully impacted by climate change. They are also among those who have contributed least to causing the crisis that is affecting them so dramatically.

As Protestant theologian Dietrich Bonhoeffer says in his *Letters and Papers from Prison,* "We have for once learnt to see the great events of world history from below, from the perspective of the outcast ... the maltreated, the powerless, the oppressed, the reviled – in short, from the perspective of those who suffer." One great gift of the human rights framework is that it gives voice to and validates the concerns of those who, due to age, circumstance, or lack of access to resources and power, need a boost for their voices to be heard. Human rights standards can advocate for the young, the vulnerable and the disenfranchised when they are most unable to advocate for themselves.

Besides these principled advantages of the human rights approach, there are also significant practical benefits to framing climate issues in human rights terms.[22] One practical advantage, for example, is that many national constitutions also include enumeration of rights, such as the right to life, to health and to a sustainable environment that can protect against climate change impacts. The rights declarations in those national constitutions can help bolster the human rights arguments. A recent United Nations report explains,

> One of the benefits of using rights-based approaches in environ-mental matters is that numerous national constitutions and laws enumerate both substantive and procedural rights that protect the environment, public health, and welfare. 78 percent of countries rec-ognize a right to life in their constitutions, and courts in at least 20 countries have held that the right to a healthy environment is implied in other constitutional rights (such as the right to life).[23]

One consequence of this is that when environmental and climate harms are linked to human rights and constitutional rights it "heightens the profile of environmental issues by connecting the importance of the environment to human well-being."[24] This just means that human beings are likely to care more about environmental and climate issues when they realize that their own well-being is directly related to how the climate is doing. If the climate system falters, so too does human thriving.

Another practical benefit according to this same UN report is that arguments based on human rights norms can be more flexible and more broadly applicable than the usual legal tactic of appealing to environmental statutes and regulatory guidelines when trying to protect the environment:

> Rights-based approaches are usually somewhat more agile and expansive than traditional regulatory and statutory approaches to environmental protection. Rights can be more broadly applicable than can statutes, which are sometimes interpreted very narrowly. Also, rights can be held collectively as well as individually, meaning that an individual or a community may be able to seek redress for an environmental harm.[25]

Yet another benefit of appealing to human rights is that human rights discourse provides an established, respected, and compelling vocabulary for addressing wrongs against people that result from government action or inaction. The combination of clear, scientifically validated facts with the genuine rhetorical power of human rights discourse can be a powerful persuader, particularly in civil society judicial settings such as People's Tribunals, People's Inquiries, and Youth Climate Courts.

The human rights framework has advantages in law as well. The United Nations report referenced above, for example, says that "Human rights have a longer history and more diverse set of treaties and institutions in place to enforce them than do environmental statutes."[26]

Further, in contrast to statutes-based approaches in which it is claimed that a specific regulatory law has been broken, "a rights-based approach can make it easier for those harmed to access courts and bring claims" because

> Most environmental *statutes* empower [governmental] agencies, not citizens, to act. By contrast, citizens usually can enforce a constitutional right because the right accrues to the individual suing, meaning it will be easier for them to access justice.[27]

A rights-based approach, therefore, puts governments in the dock rather than individuals or private corporations. It empowers individuals to sue governments that have not adequately met their human rights obligations, rather than corporations that do not currently have any such clear legal obligations.[28]

Another practical advantage of using a human rights frame is that court findings based on human rights law in one jurisdiction can potentially be of benefit to courts, law, and policy in other jurisdictions, since human rights are international and universal. Because the climate crisis is clearly an international, cross-boundary challenge, a court determination based on human rights in one country's jurisdiction may well influence similar court deliberations in a completely different jurisdiction. This means that Youth Climate Courts could potentially, over time, build a significant body of human rights jurisprudence regarding the climate obligations of local governments. The International Coalition of Youth Courts[29] will serve as the entity to hold the records for that body of jurisprudence and it may be that such a collection of human rights-based cases may even turn out to be useful when future cases are officially brought before national and international courts.

Because of all these advantages, formally pressing governments to live up to their human rights obligations turns out to be a much more powerful and effective way for young people to address the climate crisis than it would be to pressure private corporations to obey the applicable regulatory statutes. Environmentalists have spent decades suing fossil fuel corporations to force them to obey the statutes that regulate their behavior, often to little or no avail. That statutory approach has often been unhelpful for four main reasons.

1   Corporations have unfortunately been able to play an outsized role in helping to formulate the very statutes that would regulate their behavior, and thus have been able to include wording in those statutes that is favorable to their interests.
2   When corporations do get charged with violating some regulation or other, their resident legal departments have proven very effective in defending their employers against those charges, and their public relations departments have proven equally effective in redirecting public attention away from those charges.
3   Sometimes a corporation will decide it is simply more advantageous and less troublesome to just go ahead and neglect or violate a statute and then pay the resulting fines later as a simple cost of doing business.
4   And finally, regulatory statutes can vary significantly from jurisdiction to jurisdiction, some being much more favorable to industry than others, so individual corporations have become adept at taking advantage of those jurisdictional differences for their own purposes.

Industry, in other words, has figured out ways to make the statutes mostly work for them or at least to not get very much in their way. So for all these reasons it can often be to a company's great advantage if complaints against its actions are framed in terms of whether the company has obeyed or disobeyed a certain provision in a given regulatory statute.

This is not the case, though, with the rights-based approach because rights claims are much more universal, are much more applicable across jurisdictions, are sometimes also embedded in national constitutions, and because they focus on governments rather than on corporations.[30] Governments are duty-bearers when it comes to human and constitutional rights. They are obliged to respect, protect, and fulfill human rights. Corporations currently have no such clear legal obligations.

Thus the broad applicability of human rights and duties and the up-leveling of the process beyond statutes are two benefits of rights-based approaches. This may also be why the Our Children's Trust case, *Juliana v US*, and OCT's many other cases around the world have grounded their cases in constitutional- and rights-based law. That is also a reason why the Community Environmental Legal Defense Fund cases too have mostly left behind the statutory approach and switched over to focusing on the more promising community-rights approaches. These rights-based approaches recognize that it is governments who are the bearers of clear human and constitutional rights obligations, while private corporations simply are not.

The purpose of governments

We come now to the purpose of governments, what they are for, what their reason for being is, because Youth Climate Court trials will be calling governments to account for not adequately meeting their obligations as governments.

So what are governments for, exactly? What is their role in a community and what functions are they supposed to serve? The United States Declaration of Independence[31] said it pretty clearly in 1776: the purpose of governments is, first and foremost, to protect and secure the rights of the people under its care. "We hold these truths to be self-evident," it begins. We are all created equal and everyone has certain basic rights, among which are life, liberty, and the pursuit of happiness.[32]

Then, after listing those rights, comes that third sentence: "That to secure these rights, governments are instituted among men, deriving their just powers from the consent of the governed."

There it is, the purpose, the raison d'être of government is to secure the rights of its citizens. Protecting and fulfilling the rights of its people is exactly what governments are for, and if a government is not doing that, then it is not meeting its most fundamental moral obligation as a government. Governments at all levels[33] are bound by this basic obligation to protect their citizens' rights.

The UDHR agrees: "recognition of the inherent dignity and of the equal and inalienable rights of all members of the human family is the foundation of freedom, justice and peace in the world."[34] And further,

> The General Assembly ... proclaims this Universal Declaration of Human Rights as a common standard of achievement for all peoples and all nations, to the end that every individual and every organ of society ... shall strive by teaching and education to promote respect for these rights ... and by progressive measures ... to secure their universal and effective recognition and observance.[35]

Respecting people's rights, the fundamental reason for having any government, is precisely what secures freedom, justice and peace in the world. "Every organ of society[36] shall strive ... to secure the universal and effective recognition and observance" of these rights.

Human rights obligations of governments

To be more specific, a government has three primary obligations to protect people's rights and meet its primary obligations as a government. It must *respect, protect,* and *fulfill* people's rights: (1) for a government to *respect* human rights means it must refrain from taking any actions that would interfere with citizens' enjoyment of their rights. This is a negative obligation, that is, an obligation to *not* do something. The next two obligations of governments are affirmative obligations; they require governments to act, to *do* something. (2) A government's obligation to *protect* human rights means it must take measures to make sure that third parties over which the government has some authority – such as businesses, other private entities, and other governments – do not violate its citizens' rights.[37] (3) A government's duty to *fulfill* human rights means it must take active measures to ensure the realization of rights for all members of society.[38]

All three kinds of duties, to respect, protect, and fulfill, bear directly on a government's obligation to specifically secure the rights put at risk by climate change.[39] This is particularly true if that government is involved in any way with licensing, permitting, monitoring, subsidizing, or otherwise supporting fossil fuel extraction, infrastructure, distribution, or usage.

At one level it is obvious why governments should take seriously their obligation to respect, protect, and fulfill their citizens' rights: it is because that is what people need from their governments. There is another reason too, though, and that is because so many problems result when rights are not protected. The United States Declaration of Independence reminds us that if a government fails to do its job, "it is the right of the people to alter or to abolish it."[40] That means that if a government does not protect their rights, people will be inclined to get rid of that government and replace it with one that does.

The UDHR says the same thing. It is in governments' own self-interest to protect citizens' rights, it says, lest people decide to get rid of that government and replace it.[41]

So the central question on which the Youth Climate Court will be testing its local government is whether that government is or is not meeting its most fundamental moral obligation as a government.

Tools available in human rights advocacy

In their appeal to local governments to live up to their human rights obligations with respect to the climate crisis, advocates have at least three kinds of tools they can bring to bear.

Telling the story

Simple, meaningful, personal accounts of direct impacts that the climate crisis is having and will have on individuals, families, and communities can have real power. If youth witnesses tell their stories in a Youth Court trial, those stories can strengthen the prosecution's case and bring real weight to the courtroom deliberations. Personal stories have the power to simplify and clarify the issues. They can also serve to awaken people's moral imagination and evoke the compassion and outrage that will be necessary for genuine change. In a Youth Climate Court trial, witnesses will be the ones who bring the "personal narratives" perspective to the fore. Organizations such as Voice of Witness,[42] and professional storytellers can help witnesses learn how to tell their stories well and powerfully. Well-told personal accounts can serve as a major source of clarity and moral power in this work. This will be especially true if a restorative justice process is required of the government.

Some claims of injury or harm in these stories may need to be substantiated by referencing scientific studies or other testimony, and some may simply stand on their own.

Claiming moral authority with Human Rights Assessments, reports, Tribunal and Inquiry findings

Environmental Human Rights Impact Assessments[43] and human rights reports[44] from reliable national and international organizations can help clarify the moral dimensions and values at stake. They can also help identify potential legal pressure points. Foregrounding and documenting human rights standards that apply in the climate crisis can publicly clarify the injustices that follow from government inaction and can underscore the feeling of outrage experienced by those whose lives have been so negatively impacted.

Reports mentioned elsewhere in this book, such as those released by UNEP,[45] the United Nations High Commission on Human Rights,[46] the United Nations Special Rapporteur on Human Rights and the Environment,[47] and by other governmental and intergovernmental agencies, can be especially helpful to the work of Youth Climate Courts.

Exercising moral power: Inquiries, Tribunals, and Youth Climate Courts

Community-led public inquiries, such as New Zealand's "People's Inquiry into the impacts and effects of aerial pesticide spraying over urban areas of Auckland" held in 2006,[48] is one powerful tool for bringing moral pressure to bear on governments.

Public tribunals like the Permanent Peoples' Tribunal Session on Agrochemical Transnational Corporations[49] held in Bangalore, India in December 2011, and the Permanent Peoples'Tribunal Session on Human Rights, Fracking and Climate Change[50] conducted online from Oregon State University in 2018 can be both educative and empowering as well as providing resources for testimony and arguments.

Youth Climate Courts are another form of civil society, human rights court, akin in some ways to the Permanent Peoples'Tribunal in Rome, that have the power to apply significant moral pressure on local governments and require them to meet their primary obligation as governments to secure the rights of their citizens.

Since all three formats – People's Inquiries, Peoples' Tribunals and Youth Climate Courts – are community-initiated and led (not government-initiated), they can be structured to ensure that human rights standards form the ground and center of the proceedings. They can also ensure that the voices of those whose rights have been impacted are adequately heard.

The power of the moral

And finally, a reminder: large-scale shifts in public awareness and policy – which is definitely what is needed in this crisis – often come about as much for moral reasons as for economic, political, or material reasons. The French Revolution and the American Revolution, for example, the aboli-tion of slavery in the American south, the enfranchisement of women, the growing recognition of civil rights, and the ending of the Vietnam War all arose from a collective public awakening of the moral imagination. Changes of such magnitude often do not fully take hold in a society until something fundamental changes in that society's core understanding of what it considers morally acceptable and what it condemns as morally reprehensible. Youth Climate Courts, and the deep, powerful moral urgency from which they spring, can play an important role in helping effect that kind of fundamental, large-scale moral re-evaluation.

Notes

1 Stephen Humphreys, *Human Rights and Climate Change*. Cambridge University Press, 2010. Kindle Edition, location 317, first page of the Introduction.
2 "Climate Change and Human Rights." www.tribunalonfracking.org/wp-content/uploads/2015/06/UNEP-Climate-Chg-Hum-Rts-Report-12-10-15.pdf.
3 "Understanding Human Rights and Climate Change." www.tribunalonfracking.org/wp-content/uploads/2015/06/UNHCHR-Understanding-HR-CC-COP21.pdf.
4 *Safe Climate* report, p. 18.
5 "There are 195 countries in the world today. This total comprises 193 countries that are member states of the United Nations and 2 countries that are non-member observer states: the Holy See and the State of Palestine." www.worldometers.info/geography/how-many-countries-are-there-in-the-world/.
6 Quoted in Ellen Hey and Federica Violi, "The Hard Work of Regime Interaction: Climate Change and Human Rights," a paper presented at the Annual General Meeting of the Royal Netherlands Society of International Law (Preadvies Koninklijke Nederlandse Vereniging voor Internationaal Recht), 2018, p. 2.
    The authors continue: "In addition, other paragraphs of the Preamble refer to 'equitable access to sustainable development and the eradication of poverty,' 'safeguarding food security and ending hunger' and 'the imperatives of a just transition of the workforce and the creation of decent work [Paragraphs 9 and 10, Paris Agreement, respectively].' It thereby indirectly refers to a right to sustainable development, the right to food and labour rights."
7 R. Dworkin, *Taking Rights Seriously*. Cambridge, MA: Harvard University Press, 1977, pp. xi, 90.
8 United Nations General Assembly, "Universal Declaration of Human Rights," Preamble, second recital (Paris, 1948). www.un.org/en/about-us/universal-declaration-of-human-rights (accessed 8-17-21).
9 J. Morsink, *The Universal Declaration of Human Rights: Origins, Drafting and Intent*. Pennsylvania: University of Pennsylvania Press, 1999, p. 300.
10 Preamble of The Universal Declaration of Human Rights, second recital.
11 Morsink, *The Universal Declaration of Human Rights*, p. 33.
12 *Environmental Rule of Law, First Global Report*, 2019, Section 4, "Rights," p. 153. https://wedocs.unep.org/bitstream/handle/20.500.11822/27381/ERL_ch4.pdf?sequence=1&isAllowed=y (accessed 10-4-20).

13 www.environmentandhumanrights.org/resources/ccpr.pdf.
Signed by the US in 1977, ratified in 1992 and entered into force in 1992, though with some reservations on certain articles.

14 www.environmentandhumanrights.org/resources/cescr.pdf.
Signed by the US in 1977; not ratified by the US congress.

15 A set of standards is considered customary law when it has become broadly accepted, recognized, respected as legitimate and practiced more often than not around the world. According to the International Legal Research Tutorial at Duke University Law School, "The elements of customary international law include: 1) the widespread repetition by States of similar international acts over time (State practice); 2) the requirement that the acts must occur out of a sense of obligation (*opinio juris*); and 3) that the acts are taken by a significant number of States and not rejected by a significant number of States.

In 1950, the International Law Commission listed as evidence of customary international law: treaties, decisions of national courts and international tribunals, national legislation, diplomatic correspondence, opinions of national legal advisors, and the practice of international organizations." See https://law.duke.edu/ilrt/cust_law_2.htm.

16 www.mrfcj.org/principles-of-climate-justice/respect-and-protect-human-rights/.

17 For information on the UDHR see United Nations Office of the United Nations High Commissioner for Human rights, "About the Universal Declaration of Human Rights Translation Project." www.ohchr.org/En/udHr/Pages/introduction.aspx (accessed 5-7-17).

18 United Nations Office of the United Nations High Commissioner for Human Rights, "What are Human rights?" at www.ohchr.org/en/issues/pages/whatarehumanrights.aspx (accessed 8-17-21).

19 Donnelly continues: "all things considered, rights may themselves be trumped by weighty other considerations. Claiming a right, however, in effect stops the conversation and both increases and shifts the burden of proof to those who would argue that this right in this particular case is itself appropriately trumped." J. Donnelly, *Universal Human Rights in Theory and Practice*. Ithaca, NY: Cornell University Press, 2013, kindle ed., locations 227-230.

20 Dworkin, *Taking Rights Seriously*, p xi.

21 Ibid., p. 205.

22 T. Kerns, "Ten Practical Advantages of a Human Rights Approach to Environmental Advocacy," *Journal of Environmental Studies and Sciences* 3(4) (2013): 416-420.

23 *Environmental Rule of Law, First Global Report*, 2019, Section 4, "Rights," p. 147. https://wedocs.unep.org/bitstream/handle/20.500.11822/27381/ERL_ch4.pdf?sequence=1&isAllowed=y (accessed 10-4-20).

24 Ibid., pp. 137-182, p. 151.

25 Ibid., pp. 147-148.

26 Ibid., p. 141.

27 Ibid., p. 149.
28 Also – though this would not be expected to result from a Youth Climate Court – if, at some point, a human rights issue were to become a formal suit and move into the courts, and if it were to move from there into an *international* human-rights court, in those international human rights courts individual plaintiffs would have three advantages beyond what they would enjoy in domestic courts:

First, every individual person is considered to have legal standing in international human rights courts, which eliminates one of the larger obstacles to having a case heard.

Second, standards of proof in international human rights courts favor the plaintiff over the state. As Romina Picolotti and Jorge Daniel Taillant explain in their book, *Linking Human Rights and the Environment*: "unlike most national courts, the [Inter-American] Commission and Court have low standards of proof." These courts sometimes admit circumstantial evidence. This can benefit plaintiffs who often have less-than-perfect evidence to support claims of causality and health effects.

Third, the burden of proof would be on the state in such an action, rather than on the plaintiff, even though the state would be the defendant. This means that facts presented by the plaintiff would be presumed true unless proven otherwise by the state. – R. Picolotti and J. D. Taillant, *Linking Human Rights and the Environment.* Tucson: University of Arizona Press, 2003, pp. 120-134.
29 www.youthclimatecourts.org/introduction/
30 "Constitutional law and human rights law provide an important safety net when there are gaps in existing legislation." – *Environmental Rule of Law, First Global Report,* 2019, Section 4, "Rights," pp. 137-182, p. 150. https://wedocs.unep.org/bitstream/handle/20.500.11822/27381/ERL_ch4.pdf?sequence=1&isAllowed=y (accessed 10-4-20).
31 "We hold these truths to be self-evident, that all men are created equal, that they are endowed by their Creator with certain unalienable Rights, that among these are Life, Liberty and the pursuit of Happiness.– That to secure these rights, Governments are instituted among Men, deriving their just powers from the consent of the governed, – That whenever any Form of Government becomes destructive of these ends, it is the Right of the People to alter or to abolish it, and to institute new Government, laying its foundation on such principles and organizing its powers in such form, as to them shall seem most likely to effect their Safety and Happiness. Prudence, indeed, will dictate that Governments long established should not be changed for light and transient causes; and accordingly all experience hath shewn, that mankind are more disposed to suffer, while evils are sufferable, than to right themselves by abolishing the forms to which they are accustomed. But when a long train of abuses and usurpations, pursuing invariably the same Object evinces a design to reduce them under absolute Despotism, it is their right, it

is their duty, to throw off such Government, and to provide new Guards for their future security."

32 If the Declaration were written today, it would probably include other equally basic rights, such as the rights to security of person, to health, to education and several others.

33 "Constitutional and human rights are often recognized at multiple levels – subnationally, nationally, regionally, and internationally. Thus, there is typically a wider variety of remedies and fora in which to seek relief." – *Environmental Rule of Law*, First Global Report, 2019, Section 4, "Rights," p. 149. https://wedocs.unep.org/bitstream/handle/20.500.11822/27381/ERL_ch4.pdf?sequence=1&isAllowed=y (accessed 10-4-20). Further, the Permanent Peoples' Tribunal Session on Human Rights, Fracking and Climate Change ruled, in its advisory opinion, that "State and sub-state jurisdictions must … guarantee to all citizens access to justice in environmental matters, including the timely access to all relevant information, [and] the opportunity to prepare and participate in decision-making procedures" (from the court's advisory opinion, p. 60), quoted in *Bearing Witness: The Human Rights Case Against Fracking and Climate Change*. Oregon: Oregon State University Press, April 2021, p. 141.

34 Universal Declaration of Human Rights, Preamble, Recital one.

35 Ibid., Preamble.

36 Governments are clearly included as "organs of society."

37 "Governments' duties to fulfill human rights obligations include ensuring that third parties in their countries or over which they have jurisdiction respect human rights." – *Environmental Rule of Law, First Global Report*, 2019, Section 4, "Rights," p. 166.

38 United Nations Office of the High Commissioner for Human Rights, "What are human rights?" www.ohchr.org/EN/Issues/Pages/WhatareHumanRights.aspx.

39 Further, the Permanent Peoples' Tribunal Session on Human Rights, Fracking and Climate Change ruled, in its Advisory Opinion, that "State and sub-state jurisdictions must … guarantee to all citizens access to justice in environmental matters, including the timely access to all relevant information, [and] the opportunity to prepare and participate in decision-making procedures" (from the court's Advisory Opinion, p. 60), quoted in *Bearing Witness*, p. 141.

40 "That to secure these rights, Governments are instituted among Men, deriving their just powers from the consent of the governed, - That *whenever any Form of Government becomes destructive of these ends, it is the Right of the People to alter or to abolish it*, and to institute new Government, laying its foundation on such principles and organizing its powers in such form, as to them shall seem most likely to effect their Safety and Happiness. Prudence, indeed, will dictate that *Governments long established should not be changed for light and transient causes*; and accordingly all experience hath shewn that mankind are more disposed to suffer, while evils are sufferable than to right themselves by abolishing the forms to which they are accustomed."

41 "it is essential, if man is not to be compelled to have recourse, as a last resort, to rebellion against tyranny and oppression, that human rights should be protected by the rule of law." Universal Declaration of Human Rights, Preamble, third recital.

42 http://voiceofwitness.org.

43 Examples of environmental Human Rights Impact Assessments include the 2011 *Human Rights Assessment of Hydraulic Fracturing for Natural Gas in New York State.* www.tribunalonfracking.org/wp-content/uploads/2014/12/EHRA-frac-rpt-111212-1-final1.pdf; and the 2014 *Human Rights Assessment of Hydraulic Fracturing and Other Unconventional Gas Development in the United Kingdom.* www.tribunalonfracking.org/wp-content/uploads/2014/12/UK-HRIA-wo-appdx-hi-res.pdf.

44 Examples of reports on human rights and climate change would include: *Environmental Rule of Law, First Global Report,* 2019, Section 4, "Rights," pp. 137–182, https://wedocs.unep.org/bitstream/handle/20.500.11822/27381/ERL_ch4.pdf?sequence=1&isAllowed=y; and Kristen Davies et al., "'The Declaration on Human Rights and Climate Change': A New Legal Tool for Global Policy Change," *Journal of Human Rights and the Environment* 8(2) September 2017. www.tribunalonfracking.org/wp-content/uploads/2019/03/JHRE-DHRCC-article-Davies.pdf.

45 Report on Climate Change and Human Rights, United Nations Environment Programme, December 10, 2015. www.tribunalonfracking.org/wp-content/uploads/2015/06/UNEP-Climate-Chg-Hum-Rts-Report-12-10-15.pdf.

46 Understanding Human Rights and Climate Change, United Nations High Commission on Human Rights, 2015. www.tribunalonfracking.org/wp-content/uploads/2015/06/UNHCHR-Understanding-HR-CC-COP21.pdf.

47 *A Safe Climate: Human Rights and Climate Change,* October 16, 2019. Reader friendly version: http://srenvironment.org/report/a-safe-climate-human-rights-and-climate-change. Submitted to the United Nations: http://srenvironment.org/sites/default/files/Reports/2019/UNGA%20Safe%20Climate%20Report%202019.pdf.

48 J. Goven et al., "Report of the March 2006 People's Inquiry into the impacts and effects of aerial spraying pesticide over urban areas of Auckland" (The People's Inquiry Inc 2007). http://peoplesinquiry.files.wordpress.com/2013/09/web-report-finalreformatted01-1.pdf (accessed 5-30-21).

49 http://pan-international.org/wp-content/uploads/Peoples_Tribunal_on_agrochemical_TNCs_-_indictment_and_verdict.pdf.

50 www.tribunalonfracking.org.

3   Which specific human rights?

Chapter 2 provided an overview of what human rights are, where they come from, what their purposes are, and why they are so perfectly suited to serve as the deep foundation of Youth Climate Courts. The main purpose of Chapter 3, now, is to help Youth Climate Court organizers identify specific human rights that are put at risk by the climate crisis – such as the rights, especially of children, women, Indigenous peoples, and other vulnerable groups, to life, health, food, water, and a healthy environment. The information in this chapter should make it easier for prosecutors to plan their arguments, identify which rights they want to focus on, determine which witnesses they might want to seek out, and explain to others what their reasons are for deciding to organize and conduct a Youth Climate Court trial.

The role of Chapter 3 is also to help organizers locate information about each of these specific rights, discover what they include, and learn how those rights are impacted by the changing climate. This means some of the language in the following pages might be just a bit more focused than language in the first two parts, but it should still be perfectly understandable.

For each right identified below, references are provided to the human rights declarations and covenants in which that specific right has been identified and articulated. A few quotable resources are provided for each right as well. Going directly to the documents themselves, as we suggest, can also be fruitful. Finally, provisions in the Declaration on Human Rights and Climate Change (DHRCC) can also be useful in the prosecution's arguments. While the DHRCC (see Appendix I) is not itself a formally recognized international treaty (yet), its provisions do draw on and are supported by human rights instruments which are formal treaties and which are already part of customary international law.

Let us begin with a central foundational principle, that of environmental justice.

DOI: 10.4324/9781003217640-4

Environmental justice

The idea of equality before the law is at least as old as the ancient Greeks. In his famous funeral oration,[1] delivered in 431 BC, the Athenian leader Pericles laid out the importance of equal justice under law. In Athens, he bragged, "there exists equal justice to all and alike in their private disputes."[2] In our own day, the United States Supreme Court Building in Washington DC has the words "Equal Justice Under Law" inscribed over its main entrance. This fundamental right is insured in the 14th Amendment to the United States Constitution, which requires that no state shall "deny to any person within its jurisdiction the equal protection of the laws."

International human rights law concurs. Article 26 of the International Covenant on Civil and Political Rights reads:

> All persons are equal before the law and are entitled without any dis-crimination to the equal protection of the law. In this respect, the law shall prohibit any discrimination and guarantee to all persons equal and effective protection against discrimination on any ground.[3]

The International Covenant on Civil and Political Rights was signed by the US in 1977 and ratified by the United States Congress in 1992,[4] which means that its provisions (aside from certain reservations) do now have the force of domestic law in the US.[5]

The International Covenant on Economic, Social and Cultural Rights, also part of the international bill of rights, requires in Article 2.2 that governments

> guarantee that the rights enunciated in the present Covenant will be exercised without discrimination of any kind as to race, colour, sex, language, religion, political or other opinion, national or social origin, property, birth *or other status*.[6]

This same basic principle of equal justice applies with regard to envir-onmental issues just as it does to every other area of life and law. Bridget Lewis, attorney and Professor of Human Rights Law at Queensland University of Technology in Brisbane, Australia, says it very clearly:

> Environmental justice is concerned with the fair and equal distri-bution of environmental burdens and benefits at local, national and international levels. It also strives to secure the meaningful partici-pation in decision-making processes of those who are most likely to

62 *Which specific human rights?*

be affected by environmental changes which implicate them and to ensure that those who are negatively affected have adequate recourse to compensation or other remedies. Environmental injustice can therefore be identified wherever there is inequality or unfairness in the distribution of environmental burdens, where there is exclusion from the processes which determine how that distribution will be effected, or where disproportionate distribution is not balanced by sufficient reparation. This extends to potential injustices between developed and developing States, and between present and future generations.[7]

Lewis' reference to future generations, which includes today's children, is essential.

The US Environmental Protection Agency (EPA) defines environmental justice as "the fair treatment and meaningful involvement of all people regardless of race, color, national origin, or income, with respect to the development, implementation, and enforcement of environmental laws, regulations, and policies."[8] That EPA definition

was developed 25 years ago to capture the federal government's knowledge of the issue at that time and to provide an actionable definition for regulation. The environmental justice field has developed its own definitions based on people's work and life circumstances. These definitions, which capture a vision that goes beyond regulatory requirements, include:

Environmental Justice ... refers to those cultural norms and values, rules, regulations, behaviors, policies, and decisions [that] support sustainable communities where people can interact with confidence that the environment is safe, nurturing, and productive. Environmental justice is served when people can realize their highest potential ... where both cultural and biological diversity are respected and highly revered and where distributive justice prevails.
(Bunyan Bryant [italics in original])[9]

The basic principles of environmental justice thus require, in both international human rights law and in US constitutional law, that any groups or communities, including children, that are disadvantaged in any way – socially, economically, as a result of discriminatory racial policies, or disadvantaged in any other way, or who simply have less ready access to social and economic resources – be accorded the same degree of respect, fair treatment and opportunity for meaningful involvement in decision-making as groups and communities that are more advantaged and have greater access to resources. This means that no group of people, including children,[10] should bear a disproportionate share of negative environmental consequences as compared with any other group.

And yet children alive today will in fact be affected by climate change disproportionately more than will today's adults, if only because its effects are being felt earlier in their lives and during their formative years, and they will live with it longer and thus will live with its most severe effects.

The International Convention on the Rights of the Child agrees with this non-discrimination principle and insists that it is essential to insure that children not be disadvantaged in any way as a result of their status. Article 2,1, for example, requires that governments

> insure the rights [of] each child within their jurisdiction without discrimination of any kind, irrespective of the child's or his or her parent's or legal guardian's race, colour, sex, language, religion, political or other opinion, national, ethnic or social origin, property, disability, birth *or other status.*[11]

Article 3,1 further requires that

> In all actions concerning children, whether undertaken by public or private social welfare institutions, courts of law, administrative authorities or legislative bodies, the best interests of the child shall be a primary consideration.[12]

Government officials may well need to be reminded of their environmental justice obligations under both international human rights law and under United States constitutional law. Youth Climate Courts are perhaps best positioned to do that reminding. To emphasize this point in court, Youth prosecutors may decide to bring one or more witnesses to testify to ways in which children are being, and will continue to be, subjected to a disproportionate and unfair share of negative consequences resulting from the climate crisis.

Right to life

The right to life is one of the unalienable rights underscored in the United States Declaration of Independence and, as of 2006, "144 of the world's countries recognized the right to life in their constitutions."[13] So the right to life is an example of a human right that is also a constitutional right in 78 percent of the world's countries. Further, the right to life is recognized as a basic right in several international human rights covenants and declarations as well.[14]

The 2019 *Safe Climate* report prepared by the United Nations Special Rapporteur on Human Rights and the Environment states clearly and unambiguously that

> The right to life is universally recognized in human rights law. In 2018, the Human Rights Committee stated that "environmental degradation, climate change and unsustainable development constitute some of the most pressing and serious threats to the ability of present and future generations to enjoy the right to life."[15] In order to uphold the right to life, States have an obligation to take effective measures to mitigate climate change, enhance the adaptive capacity of vulnerable populations and prevent foreseeable loss of life.[16]

The right to life, perhaps the most basic of human rights, is affirmed directly in the Universal Declaration of Human Rights and in the International Covenant on Civil and Political Rights, both part of the International Bill of Rights.

> Universal Declaration of Human Rights, Article 3. "Everyone has the right to life, liberty and security of person."[17]
> International Covenant on Civil and Political Rights, Article 6. "Every human being has the inherent right to life."[18]

The right to life imposes a positive obligation on States to protect citizens from conditions that would threaten their lives. When governments permit circumstances that entail a clear threat to life, they have failed to protect this right.

Known consequences of anthropogenic climate change – such as droughts, flooding, wildfires and large-scale food and water insecurity – undermine citizens' right to life. A government's failure to do its part in guarding against and mitigating these consequences constitutes a miscarriage of the government's duty to uphold this right.

As environmental human rights scholar and attorney Bridget Lewis explains,

> [T]he effects of climate change threaten the right to life in a number of ways, both directly and indirectly. The Intergovernmental Panel on Climate change (IPCC) projects with confidence that climate change will cause a number of potentially life-threatening environmental impacts, including heatwaves and drought, storms and cyclones, heavy precipitation events and longer monsoon seasons, leading to more frequent flooding (Alexander et al. 2013; Field et al.

2014). It is predicted that these changes will increase the number of persons suffering from death, disease and injury (Huant et al. 2011; Hajat et al. 2014). The World Health Organization has predicted that between 2030 and 2050, climate change will account for approximately an additional 250,000 deaths each year.

Climate change will also impact on the right to life through "an increase in hunger and malnutrition and related disorders impacting on child growth and development: cardiorespiratory morbidity and mortality related to ground-level ozone." Particular communities also face specific threats …. [F]or example, diminishing sea ice presents a serious risk of injury and death for Arctic communities who regularly travel across the ice.

Climate change is also predicted to exacerbate weather-related disasters, which already kill thousands of people each year. Destructive events such as heatwaves, storms, and floods have the effect of arbitrarily depriving people of their life and thereby undermine the right to life. Further, [there is also the] potential for climate change to exacerbate other life-threatening problems such as malnutrition and epidemics.[19]

The 2015 United Nations report, Climate Change and Human Rights, explains further that

It is now beyond dispute that climate change caused by human activity has negative impacts on the full enjoyment of human rights. Climate change has profound impacts on a wide variety of human rights, including the rights to life, self-determination, development, food, health, water and sanitation and housing. The human rights framework also requires that global efforts to mitigate and adapt to climate change should be guided by relevant human rights norms and principles including the rights to participation and information, transparency, accountability, equity, and non-discrimination. Simply put, *climate change is a human rights problem and the human rights framework must be part of the solution.* [20]

The United Nations Environment Programme has also issued strong warnings about the dangers of climate change and its implications for the right to life:[21]

The impacts of climate change on freshwater resources, ecosystems, and human settlements are already undermining access to clean water, food, shelter, and other basic human needs; interfering with livelihoods; and displacing people from their homes. Even if we remain within the international goal of 2°C of global warming, these impacts will expand dramatically in the coming decades.

These impacts constitute a serious interference with the exercise of fundamental human rights, such as the rights to life, health, water, food, housing, and an adequate standard of living.

Mitigation, adaptation, and geoengineering measures can also adversely affect the exercise of human rights. For example, there are documented instances of hydroelectric and biofuel projects that have resulted in human rights violations. There is also a high risk of human rights violations resulting from the implementation of resettlement programs for those who are displaced or at risk of displacement due to climate change, and a corresponding need to ensure that such programs are undertaken with adequate input and consent from those who are relocated.[22]

Right to health

The human health impacts of climate change have already begun to take their toll. The American Medical Association, the American College of Physicians, and the British Medical Association all formally recognized in 2019 that climate change is a global health emergency: "The World Health Organisation has recognised since 2015 that climate change is the greatest threat to global health in the 21st century, and argued the scientific evidence for that assessment is 'overwhelming.'"[23] The Australian Medical Association president has said,

> Climate change will cause higher mortality and morbidity from heat stress … Climate change will cause injury and mortality from increasingly severe weather events. Climate change will cause increases in the transmission of vector-borne diseases. Climate change will cause food insecurity resulting from declines in agricultural outputs. Climate change will cause a higher incidence of mental ill-health. These effects are already being observed internationally and in Australia.[24]

Even a brief listing of climate change impacts on human health would need to include direct and indirect effects resulting from excess heat, droughts, storms, warmer and wetter climates, wildfires, warmer freshwater, and so on. These environmental conditions have profound impacts on human nutrition, on diseases such as heat stress, malaria, dengue fever, tick-borne illnesses, mental health, and so on, and on infectious diseases such as Covid-19.[25]

In February of 2020, over 500 Oregon state health professionals and organizations declared, "We believe that all people, including future generations, have the right to the environmental, economic and social resources needed to live healthy and productive lives."[26]

In fact, the right of everyone to live in conditions conducive to the highest standard of health is specifically articulated in several human rights instruments including, among others, the Universal Declaration of Human Rights, the International Covenant on Economic, Social and Cultural Rights, the Aarhus Convention, the Convention on the Rights of the Child and the United Nations Declaration on the Rights of Indigenous Peoples:

> Universal Declaration of Human Rights, Article 25
> "Everyone has the right to a standard of living adequate for the health and well-being of himself and of his family, including food, clothing, housing and medical care"[27]
> International Covenant on Economic, Social and Cultural Rights, Article 12.
> "States Parties to the present Covenant recognize the right of everyone to the enjoyment of the highest attainable standard of physical and mental health."[28]
> Convention on the Rights of the Child, Article 24.
> "States Parties recognize the right of the child to the enjoyment of the highest attainable standard of health."[29]
> Aarhus Convention, Preamble.
> "Every person has the right to live in an environment adequate to his or her health and well-being, and the duty, both individually and in association with others, to protect and improve the environment for the benefit of present and future generations."[30]
> United Nations Declaration on the Rights of Indigenous Peoples, 24 (2).
> "Indigenous individuals have an equal right to the enjoyment of the highest attainable standard of physical and mental health."[31]

These human rights instruments all recognize the right of everyone, especially children, Indigenous persons, and other groups facing increased vulnerabilities, to live in safe and healthy conditions, including safe and healthy environmental conditions, and not to be forced involuntarily to suffer exposure to conditions that adversely affect their health.

Enabling practices or conditions that put anyone – especially children, Indigenous persons, or other vulnerable groups – at increased risk of adverse health effects would be an encroachment on the right to health.

The United Nations *Safe Climate* report makes it very clear that "adverse health impacts" resulting from climate change include

> not only premature deaths but also increased incidences of respiratory disease, cardiovascular disease, malnutrition, stunting, wasting, allergies, heat stroke, injuries, water-borne and vector-borne diseases and mental illness. Dengue fever is the most rapidly spreading vector-borne disease, with a thirtyfold increase in global incidence that is largely attributable to climate change. Hundreds of millions of people are exposed to extreme weather events annually, resulting in injuries, illnesses and mental health impacts. Climate change also erodes many of the key social and environmental determinants of health, including access to adequate food and water, clean air, culture and livelihoods. Health is also affected by climate-related displacement, migration and reduced access to health-care services.[32]

Youth Climate Court prosecutors who choose to include the right to health in their arguments will find that concerns about human health effects do resonate with people, probably because so many people have close experience, either in their own bodies or those of people close to them, with the toll that ill health can take on a person's life and well-being.

Right to an adequate standard of living

The right of all human beings to an adequate standard of living is recognized in the Universal Declaration of Human Rights, in the International Covenant on Economic, Social and Cultural Rights, and in the Convention on the Rights of the Child.

> Universal Declaration of Human Rights, Article 25, 1.
> "Everyone has the right to a standard of living adequate for the health and well-being of himself and of his family, including food, clothing, housing and medical care and necessary social services."[33]
> International Covenant on Economic, Social and Cultural Rights, Article 11.
> "The States Parties to the present Covenant recognize the right of everyone to an adequate standard of living for himself and his family, including adequate food, clothing and housing"[34]
> Convention on the Rights of the Child Article, 24, 2 (c).
> "States Parties ... shall take appropriate measures ... To combat disease and malnutrition ... through the provision of adequate nutritious foods and clean drinking-water, taking into consideration the dangers and risks of environmental pollution."[35]

The right to an adequate standard of living means that all persons and families are guaranteed access to the basic preconditions for a healthy life including but not limited to: secure access to nourishing food, clean water, shelter from the elements, and adequate clothing. This right requires governments to take positive action to prevent conditions that would hinder citizens' access to these fundamentals, including taking measures against environmental pollution, the spread of disease, and malnutrition.

According to Article 11 of the International Covenant on Economic, Social, and Cultural Rights, all persons are entitled to an adequate standard of living for themselves and their families including adequate housing. The United Nations High Commission for Human Rights clarifies what this means in the context of the climate crisis.

Climate change threatens the right to housing in a number of ways. Extreme weather events can destroy homes displacing multitudes of people. Drought, erosion and flooding can gradually render territories [un]inhabitable resulting in displacement and migration. Sea level rise threatens the very land upon which houses in low-lying areas are situated and is expected to "continue for centuries even if the global mean temperature is stabilized." ...

According to World Bank reports, climate change will cause "health impacts [that] are likely to increase and be exacerbated by high rates of malnutrition", including potential increases in vector-borne diseases and "heat-amplified levels of smog [that] could exacerbate respiratory disorders." In its most recent report, the IPCC found that "climate change is expected to lead to increases in ill-health in many regions and especially in developing countries with low income, as compared to a baseline without climate change." ...

Although the right to water is not explicitly recognized in the [International Covenant on Economic, Social, and Cultural Rights], General Comment No. 15 of the Committee on Economic, Social and Cultural Rights articulates this right stating: "The human right to water entitles everyone to sufficient, safe, acceptable, physically accessible and affordable water for personal and domestic uses." In its resolution 64/292, the General Assembly recognised "the right to safe and clean drinking water and sanitation as a human right that is essential for the full enjoyment of life and all human rights." The right to water and sanitation is also found in legal instruments such as the Convention on the Elimination of Discrimination against Women (CEDAW), among others. Pursuant to General Comment 15, "States parties have to adopt effective measures to realize, without discrimination, the right to water." ...

According to the IPCC, "climate change is projected to reduce renewable surface water and groundwater resources in most dry subtropical regions ... intensifying competition for water." The IPCC further found that climate change will likely increase the risk of water scarcity in urban areas and "rural areas are expected to experience major impacts on water availability and supply." According to a recent World Bank report, a two-degree Celsius average global increase in temperature may result in one to two billion no longer having enough water to meet their needs. Reduced access to water will disproportionately impact persons, groups and peoples in vulnerable situations. For example, reduced access to water introduces added burdens for women and girls in developing countries, who are often responsible for fetching water for their families from distant sources and have distinct needs for water and sanitation. ...

States have an obligation to respect, protect, fulfil and promote all human rights for all persons without discrimination. Failure to take affirmative measures to prevent human rights harms caused by climate change, including foreseeable long-term harms, breaches this obligation. The Fifth Report of the Intergovernmental Panel on Climate Change confirms that climate change is caused by anthropogenic emissions of greenhouse gases. Among other impacts, climate change negatively affects people's rights to health, housing, water and food. These negative impacts will increase exponentially according to the degree of climate change that ultimately takes place and will disproportionately affect individuals, groups and peoples in vulnerable situations including, women, children, older persons, indigenous peoples, minorities, migrants, rural workers, persons with disabilities and the poor. Therefore, States must act to limit anthropogenic emissions of greenhouse gases [by working to mitigate climate change, for example], including through regulatory measures, in order to prevent to the greatest extent possible the current and future negative human–rights impacts of climate change.[36]

Right to food

The 2019 *Safe Climate* report issued by the United Nations Special Rapporteur on Human Rights and the Environment makes clear that the right to food is formally declared in both the Universal Declaration of Human Rights and in the International Covenant on Economic, Social and Cultural Rights:

> The Universal Declaration of Human Rights and the International Covenant on Economic, Social and Cultural Rights include food as

part of the right to an adequate standard of living, with the Covenant referring to the "fundamental right of everyone to be free from hunger."

Food production, food security and the enjoyment of the right to food are affected by shifting precipitation patterns, higher temperatures, extreme weather events, changing sea ice conditions, droughts, floods, algal blooms and salinization. Changes in climate are already undermining the production of major crops, such as wheat, rice and maize. Without adaptation, or where adaptations fall short, this is expected to worsen as temperatures increase and become more extreme. In the oceans, temperature changes, bleaching of coral reefs and ocean acidification are affecting fisheries. Climate change also exacerbates drivers of food insecurity and malnutrition, such as conflict and poverty.[37]

This is important because, as Professor Bridget Lewis explains in *Environmental Human Rights and Climate Change*, food security is expected to be put increasingly at risk in a climate-changed world:

It is predicted that climate change will impact on food production, availability and stability in a number of ways. Production and availability of food will be affected directly through changes in agroecological conditions.[38]

Climate change is also likely to affect food security indirectly by destabilizing access to food. Local food supplies will become more susceptible to interruptions due to extreme weather events, especially floods and droughts. Prices of food are also likely to rise under climate change due to problems of supply and increased costs of transportation. ...

The right to food is also at risk from actions taken in the pursuit of climate change mitigation and adaptation. For example, mitigation efforts aimed at reducing greenhouse gas emissions might involve greater production of biofuels as a source of renewable energy. Where this requires changes to land use, agricultural production for food may be diminished. ...

Overall, the World Food Programme has predicted that by 2050, the number of people at risk of hunger as a result of climate change will increase by 10-20% more than would be the case in a world free of climate change, and that the number of malnourished children is expected to increase by 24 million.[39]

We are seeing increasing instances of the climate crisis endangering food security. A recent news story reports that unusual climate conditions are contributing to a catastrophic outbreak of locusts in Africa. A *New York Times* article explained: "The outbreak is making the region's bad food security situation worse, the United Nations' Food and Agriculture Organization has warned. Hundreds of thousands of acres of crops have been destroyed." It went on to say,

> The most serious outbreak of locusts in 25 years is spreading across East Africa and posing an unprecedented threat to food security in some of the world's most vulnerable countries, authorities say. Unusual climate conditions are partly to blame. ...
>
> An "extremely dangerous increase" in locust swarm activity has been reported in Kenya, the East African regional body reported this week. One swarm measured 60 kilometers (37 miles) long by 40 kilometers (25 miles) wide in the country's northeast, the Intergovernmental Authority on Development said in a statement.
>
> "A typical desert locust swarm can contain up to 150 million locusts per square kilometer", it said. "Swarms migrate with the wind and can cover 100 to 150 kilometers in a day. An average swarm can destroy as much food crops in a day as is sufficient to feed 2,500 people."[40]

Examples like this represent other ways – in addition to droughts, floods, wildfires, water scarcity, sea-level rise, saltwater incursion, and so on – the climate crisis puts food security at serious risk.[41]

Right to water and sanitation

The United Nations High Commission for Human Rights explains in its 2015 Report, *Understanding Human Rights and Climate Change*, that the right to water is defined as "the right of everyone to sufficient, safe, acceptable and physically accessible and affordable water for personal and domestic uses."[42]

The right to safe and clean drinking water is explicitly articulated in United Nations Resolution 64/292 where it is recognized as essential to the realization of all other human rights. The right to water is also expressed directly in the Convention on the Elimination of All Forms of Discrimination Against Women and in the Convention on the Rights of the Child. It is also clearly implied as essential to the realization of the right to health articulated in the Universal Declaration of Human Rights, in the International Covenant on Economic, Social and Cultural Rights, and in the United Nations Declaration on the Rights of Indigenous Peoples.

United Nations Resolution 64/292.

"The General Assembly … recognizes the right to safe and clean drinking water and sanitation as a human right that is essential for the full enjoyment of life and all human rights."[43]

Convention on the Elimination of All Forms of Discrimination Against Women, Article 14 (h).

"The right to enjoy adequate living conditions, particularly in relation to housing, sanitation, electricity and water supply …"[44]

Convention on the Rights of the Child, Article 24 (c).

"States Parties recognize the right of the child to the enjoyment of the highest attainable standard of health …" Also "States Parties shall … take appropriate measures (c) To combat disease and malnutrition … through the provision of adequate nutritious foods and clean drinking-water, taking into consideration the dangers and risks of environmental pollution."[45]

Universal Declaration of Human Rights, Article 25 (1).

"Everyone has the right to a standard of living adequate for the health and well-being of himself and of his family, including food, clothing, housing and medical care."[46]

International Covenant on Economic, Social and Cultural Rights, Article 12.

"States Parties to the present Covenant recognize the right of everyone to the enjoyment of the highest attainable standard of physical and mental health."[47]

United Nations Declaration on the Rights of Indigenous Peoples, 24 (2).

"Indigenous individuals have an equal right to the enjoyment of the highest attainable standard of physical and mental health."[48]

The 2019 *Safe Climate* report issued by the UN Special Rapporteur on Human Rights and the Environment explains how the right to water and sanitation are impacted by climate change:

Climate change is affecting precipitation patterns across the world, with some dry areas receiving less precipitation and wet areas receiving more frequent and intense precipitation. The four key elements of the rights to water and sanitation are threatened: availability, accessibility, acceptability and quality. The Intergovernmental Panel on Climate Change warned of particularly high vulnerability to water stress in small island developing States and parts of Africa, Asia and Latin America. Climate change has already contributed to a water crisis in the Plurinational State of Bolivia, where glaciers are receding and water rationing has been required in major cities. Indigenous pastoralists in Turkana County, Kenya, are struggling because climate change is negatively affecting water supplies, grazing opportunities and livestock herds, and increasing competition, conflict and insecurity.[49] Turkana women and girls bear the burden of longer walks to obtain potable water.

The right to sanitation may be threatened when water is increasingly scarce, and when floods, intense precipitation or other extreme weather events damage infrastructure or impair access. The rise in extreme weather events owing to climate change increases the risk of water-borne diseases, including typhoid fever and cholera.[50]

Professor Bridget Lewis continues this argument. In *Environmental Human Rights and Climate Change,* she writes,

> The complexity of our relationship with water, which is both a basic necessity for life as well as an essential requirement for agriculture and many industrial processes, means that the pressure placed on water supplies by climate change has the potential to impact in a number of negative ways ... Northern Hemisphere spring snow cover and glacier volumes will significantly decrease. These changes to the cryosphere are projected to negatively affect water availability for more than one-sixth of the world's population supplied by such water from mountain ranges. Water supplies will also be affected by weather extremes such as floods and droughts, and salt-water inundation due to storm surges and sea-level rise.[51]

Rights of the child

The United Nations Convention on the Rights of the Child (CRC or UNCRC) is one of the most important international human rights treaties for addressing the rights of children (i.e., all persons under 18). Though the United States has only signed but not ratified this convention,[52] "One hundred and ninety states (of the world's one hundred ninety-five) have agreed to become parties to the Convention on the Rights of the Child, giving it the distinction of being the most widely ratified treaty in the history of the world."[53] Governments that have signed and ratified this treaty have promised

> to ensure the child such protection and care as is necessary for his or her well-being, taking into account the rights and duties of his or her parents, legal guardians, or other individuals legally responsible for

him or her, and, to this end, shall take all appropriate legislative and administrative measures.[54]

They also promise to "undertake all appropriate legislative, administrative, and other measures for the implementation of the rights recognized in the present Convention."[55] One of the rights recognized in the CRC that is particularly relevant to Youth Climate Court organizers insures that "the child who is capable of forming his or her own views [has] the right to express those views freely in all matters affecting the child,"[56] and also that "the child shall in particular be provided the opportunity to be heard in any judicial and administrative proceedings affecting the child."[57]

The climate crisis, as we have seen, clearly affects children and young people. The United Nations *Safe Climate* report underscores the importance of recognizing the rights of children and how seriously those rights are impacted by the climate crisis:

The Convention on the Rights of the Child, in describing the right to health, explicitly requires that States act in the best interests of the child and consider "the dangers and risks of environmental pollution." Children and young people around the world are increasingly outspoken about the impacts of climate change on their rights and their future and the need for urgent action.[58] In response to the call for inputs for the present report, one indigenous youth leader observed that "Earth is a giving planet ... Everything we ever needed to live, to survive, to enjoy the wonders of the world was provided by nature, yet we humans have become the most dangerous threat to life on Earth."

Children are particularly vulnerable to health problems exacerbated by climate change, including vector-borne diseases, malnutrition, acute respiratory infections, diarrhoea and other waterborne illnesses.[59] Extreme weather events pose unique threats to the health and well-being of young bodies and minds. Globally, over 500 million children live in high or extremely high drought severity zones and 115 million are at high risk from tropical cyclones. By 2040, almost 600 million children will live in regions with extremely limited water resources. The United Nations Children's Fund warns that "climate change will harm the poorest and most vulnerable children first, hardest and longest."[60]

The United Nations Convention on the Rights of the Child is an eminently readable document and Youth Climate Court organizers will find much in it that is quotable and to their liking. If organizers decide to read through any of the relevant human rights documents mentioned in this book, the Universal Declaration of Human Rights and the Convention on the Rights of the Child would certainly be two of the more relevant.

And finally, especially relevant for governments in the Americas, the American Convention on Human Rights[61] adds one more confirmation of these rights in its Article 19 on the rights of the child: "Every minor child has the right to the measures of protection required by his condition as a minor on the part of his family, society, and the state."

The responsibility of governments to protect children from the impacts of the climate crisis, especially from those impacts that are so eminently foreseeable, is clearly underscored in this provision.

Rights of vulnerable populations

Vulnerable populations are communities of people who are socially, economically, politically, institutionally, or culturally marginalized. Due to their underprivileged positions, they contribute the least to causing the climate crisis. However, by the nature of their subsistence, occupations, lack of resources, and other factors, they are more vulnerable than most and they stand to disproportionately bear more severe impacts of climate change.

The United Nations *Safe Climate* report underscores how much more dramatically the risks and costs of the climate crisis are borne by these marginalized and vulnerable people and communities, despite their having contributed so little to causing the crisis. In the following passage, the *Safe Climate* report describes impacts on the vulnerable populations of women, Indigenous peoples, and persons with disabilities:

> In 2018, the Committee on the Elimination of Discrimination against Women recognized that climate change impacts, including disasters, have a disproportionate effect on women.[62] Women experience greater financial and resource constraints, lower levels of access to information, and less decision-making authority in their homes, communities and countries.[63] In its recommendations to States (concluding observations), the Committee has repeatedly urged States to take into account the greater vulnerability of women by adopting a human rights-based approach to all decisions related to adaptation, mitigation, disaster risk reduction and climate finance.[64] The Committee has made specific recommendations regarding older women and rural women, two groups with particular vulnerabilities to climate change.[65] Women are also leaders and vital agents of change, maximizing use of their knowledge and resources to help families to adapt.[66]

Despite contributing little to the problem, roughly 400 million indigenous peoples around the world are especially vulnerable to climate change because of their close connection to nature and dependence on wildlife, plants and healthy ecosystems for food, medicine and cultural needs. On the other hand, indigenous people can make important contributions to solutions, through traditional knowledge, legal systems and cultures that have proven effective at conserving land, water, biodiversity and ecosystems, including forests.[67]

Persons with disabilities could also be disproportionately affected by climate change. The Committee on the Rights of Persons with Disabilities emphasized that States must ensure that the requirements of all persons with disabilities are taken into consideration when designing and implementing adaptation and disaster risk reduction measures.[68,69]

The right of Indigenous peoples to own, use, develop, and control traditional lands and water

Recognizing the unique conditions faced by Indigenous peoples around the world, the United Nations Declaration on the Rights of Indigenous Peoples (UNDRIP), many years in the making, was finally officially adopted by the UN in 2007. This document addresses challenges specific to Indigenous peoples and also recognizes certain rights due to the community itself as a rights-bearing entity. The community is not recognized as a rights-bearing entity in most other human rights instruments, focused as they are on the rights of individual persons. In this Declaration, though, tribal communities are also recognized as rights-holders along with the individual members of those communities. Several of the rights underscored in UNDRIP also recognize the intimate connections tribal communities have with their ancestral lands, protecting those lands as a matter of rights. These protections "are critical to indigenous peoples and persons, who are often closely tied economically and culturally to the environment and natural resources and who are often disenfranchised from modern political and legal systems."[70]

One of those rights, the right of Indigenous peoples to own, use, develop, and control their traditional lands and resources (including water) is especially important. This means that those communities have the final say in determining what is best for them. That right is recognized by Articles 26, 29 and 32 of the UNDRIP.

United Nations Declaration on the Rights of Indigenous Peoples, Article 26.[71]

"Indigenous peoples have the right to the lands, territories and resources which they have traditionally owned, occupied or otherwise used or acquired."

"Indigenous peoples have the right to own, use, develop and control the lands, territories and resources that they possess by reason of traditional ownership or other traditional occupation or use, as well as those which they have otherwise acquired."

"States shall give legal recognition and protection to these lands, territories and resources. Such recognition shall be conducted with due respect to the customs, traditions and land tenure systems of the indigenous peoples concerned."

United Nations Declaration on the Rights of Indigenous Peoples, Article 29.[72]

"Indigenous peoples have the right to the conservation and protection of the environment and the productive capacity of their lands or territories and resources. States shall establish and implement assistance programmes for indigenous peoples for such conservation and protection, without discrimination."

"States shall take effective measures to ensure that no storage or disposal of hazardous materials shall take place in the lands or territories of indigenous peoples without their free, prior and informed consent."

"States shall also take effective measures to ensure, as needed, that programmes for monitoring, maintaining and restoring the health of indigenous peoples, as developed and implemented by the peoples affected by such materials, are duly implemented."

United Nations Declaration on the Rights of Indigenous Peoples, Article 32.[73]

"Indigenous peoples have the right to determine and develop priorities and strategies for the development or use of their lands or territories and other resources."

"States shall consult and cooperate in good faith with the indigenous peoples concerned through their own representative institutions in order to obtain their free and informed consent prior to the approval of any project affecting their lands or territories and other resources, particularly in connection with the development, utilization or exploitation of mineral, water or other resources."

"States shall provide effective mechanisms for just and fair redress for any such activities, and appropriate measures shall be taken to mitigate adverse environmental, economic, social, cultural or spiritual impact."

The Inter-American Court of Human Rights has interpreted this to mean that "Indigenous groups, by the fact of their very existence, have the right to live freely in their own territory. The close ties of indigenous people with the land," the court said,

> must be recognized and understood as the fundamental basis of their cultures, their spiritual life, their integrity and their economic survival. For indigenous communities, relations to the land are not merely a matter of possession and production but a material and spiritual element which they must fully enjoy, even to preserve their cultural legacy and transmit it to future generations.[74]

When climate change undermines Indigenous peoples' ability to live on traditional territories, to rely on traditional means of subsistence and travel, and to enjoy cultural practices related to their land, then this right has been violated.[75]

Right to a healthy environment

Climate disruption clearly threatens the right to a healthy environment. Fortunately, countries around the world are beginning to acknowledge the right to a healthy environment as a constitutional or statutory right. The "Environmental Rule of Law" defines this right:

> This right asserts that the environment must meet certain basic benchmarks of healthfulness and includes affirmative substantive rights, such as the right to clean air and water, and defensive substantive rights, such as the right to be free from toxic wastes or pollution.[76]

The *Safe Climate* report concurs:

> As noted in the Special Rapporteur's previous reports, the right to a safe, clean, healthy and sustainable environment is recognized in law by at least 155 Member States.[77] The substantive elements of this right include a safe climate, clean air, clean water and adequate sanitation, healthy and sustainably produced food, non-toxic environments in which to live, work, study and play, and healthy biodiversity and ecosystems. These elements are informed by commitments made under international environmental treaties, such as the United Nations Framework Convention on Climate Change, wherein States pledged to "prevent dangerous anthropogenic interference with the climate system," or in other words to maintain a safe climate.[78]

Also, at the international level, the right to a healthy and sustainable environment is recognized in the Preamble of the Aarhus Convention:

> Every person has the right to live in an environment adequate to his or her health and well-being, and the duty, both individually and in association with others, to protect and improve the environment for the benefit of present and future generations.[79]

That climate change poses such serious threats to human rights and even to human survival was recognized by the judges' Advisory Opinion in the Permanent Peoples' Tribunal 2018 Session on Human Rights, Fracking and Climate Change.[80] There the judges highlighted the DHRCC and cited several DHRCC provisions, including Article 4,

> All human beings have the right to a planetary climate suitable to meet equitably the ecologically responsible needs of present generations without impairing the rights of future generations to meet equitably their ecologically responsible needs.[81]

The 2015 Climate Change and Human Rights report prepared by the United Nations Environment Programme, fully agrees and provides a detailed account:

> It has long been recognized that a clean, healthy and functional environment is integral to the enjoyment of human rights, such as the rights to life, health, food and an adequate standard of living. Anthropogenic climate change is the largest, most pervasive threat to the natural environment and human societies the world has ever experienced. The latest assessment report from the Intergovernmental Panel on Climate Change (IPCC) describes how observed and predicted changes in climate will adversely affect billions of people and the ecosystems, natural resources, and physical infrastructure upon which they depend. These harmful impacts include sudden-onset events that pose a direct threat to human lives and safety, as well as more gradual forms of environmental degradation that will undermine access to clean water, food, and other key resources that support human life.
> *Terrestrial Ecosystems.* Even under the intermediate emissions scenarios there is a "high risk" that climate change will cause "abrupt and irreversible regional-scale change in the composition, structure, and function of terrestrial and freshwater ecosystems" in this century. [T]he IPCC predicts that climate change will "reduce the

populations, vigor, and viability" of many species, especially those with spatially restricted populations, and will increase the extinction risk for many species.

Increased tree death has been observed in many places worldwide, and there is high confidence that this can be attributed to climate change in some regions. "Forest dieback" is a major environmental risk, which has potentially significant impacts on climate, biodiversity, water quality, wood production, and livelihoods. The drivers of tree death include high temperatures and drought, and changes in the abundance of insect pests and pathogens (related, in part, to warming).

Ocean Systems. Climate change is altering the physical, chemical, and biological properties of the ocean; scientists have already observed large-scale distribution shifts of species and altered ecosystem composition as a result of ocean warming....

According to IPCC projections, climate change will significantly reduce surface water and groundwater resources in most dry subtropical regions, thus intensifying competition for water among agriculture, ecosystems, settlements, industry, and energy production, and affecting regional water, energy, and food security. Climate change will also increase the frequency of droughts in presently dry areas....

Adaptation. One concern is that some adaptation programs, may benefit one group to the detriment of another – as might be the case for coastal fortifications that protect one community while exposing another to greater risk of erosion and/or flooding. There is also the risk that adaptation measures will be undertaken without the necessary public consultation and may result in outcomes that adversely affect the very persons they aim to protect. There is a risk of human-rights violations in the context of relocation and resettlement programs, and a corresponding need to ensure that such programs are undertaken with adequate input and consent from those who are relocated. It should be noted that both the Adaptation Fund and the Green Climate Fund have put in place environmental and social safeguards. ...

Geoengineering. Although there have not yet been any significant field tests of geoengineering technology, far less any large-scale geoengineering projects, it is important to note that such projects could seriously interfere with the enjoyment of human rights for millions and perhaps billions of people. For example, one recent study of five potential geoengineering methods deployed in high greenhouse gas emissions scenarios concluded that these methods could severely disrupt ocean and terrestrial ecosystems. These disruptive effects could undermine the provision of ecosystem goods and services, thus interfering with access to food, clean water, and other key resources. Another study found that proposals for solar radiation management would cause widespread regional-scale changes in precipitation. Such shifts could lead to increases in storms and flooding in some areas and drought in others, with adverse impacts on natural ecosystems and human settlements. In addition, there is at this time no mechanism in place to ensure that governments or private parties carrying out geoengineering projects coordinate with the international community, or even disclose information to and allow for public participation.[82]

All this was confirmed again in 2016 when United States federal Judge Ann Aiken wrote in her opinion in *Juliana v. USA et al.* that "the right to a climate system capable of sustaining human life is fundamental to a free and ordered society."[83]

Importantly, the Preamble of the United States Constitution makes it clear that one of the central purposes of this form of government is to "secure the Blessings of Liberty to ourselves and our Posterity."[84] What Judge Aiken makes clear here is that enjoying the blessings of liberty will not be possible for "ourselves and our Posterity" unless there exists a sustainable environment to enjoy them in.

Human rights documents

Youth Climate Court organizers will want to know that these human rights documents are not difficult to read so there is no reason to feel intimidated by them. Most of these documents have little use for the lawyerly gobbledygook that so often shows up in statutes, ordinances and rules created by legislatures, city councils, and other government bodies. These human rights documents are intended to be read by ordinary people – the rights-holders – not just by lawyers and government officials. Here, for example is the whole of Article 3 in the Universal Declaration of Human Rights: "Everyone has the right to life, liberty and security of person." And here is the entirety of Article 6 in the Convention on the Rights of the Child: "1. States Parties [i.e., governments] recognize that every child has the inherent right to life. 2. States Parties shall ensure to the maximum extent possible the survival and development of the child."

A good collection of environmentally relevant human rights documents, including most of those mentioned above, can be found on the Resources page of the YouthClimateCourts.org website.[85] Virtually all human rights documents and instruments are available online in the collection of the University of Minnesota Human Rights Library,[86] and a web search will show that many are also readily available at other locations on the web.

For quick reference, here are a few of the human rights instruments and United Nations reports frequently referenced in this book.

Human rights instruments:

- The Universal Declaration of Human Rights[87]
- The Convention on the Rights of the Child[88]
- The Convention on the Elimination of All Forms of Discrimination Against Women[89]
- The United Nations Declaration on the Rights of Indigenous Peoples.[90]

United Nations reports on human rights and climate change:

- *A Safe Climate: Human Rights and Climate Change*, United Nations Special Rapporteur on Human Rights and the Environment, 2019[91]
- Understanding Human Rights and Climate Change, United Nations High Commissioner for Human Rights, 2015[92]
- Report on Human Rights and Climate Change, United Nations Environment Programme, 2015.[93]

Notes

1 Thucydides, Pericles' Funeral Oration. http://hrlibrary.umn.edu/education/thucydides.html (accessed 3-11-20).
2 http://hrlibrary.umn.edu/education/thucydides.html.
3 www.environmentandhumanrights.org/resources/ccpr.pdf.
4 The University of Minnesota Human Rights Library maintains a record of which countries have signed and ratified which human rights treaties. To see which human rights documents your country has signed visit http://hrlibrary.umn.edu/research/ratification-index.html (accessed 20-10-20).
5 The International Covenant on Civil and Political Rights entered into force internationally on March 23, 1976. It was signed by the US in 1977, ratified in 1992 and entered into force in the US in 1992 (with reservations on articles 5–7, 10(2,3), 15(1), 19, 20, 27 and 47, and formal understandings on articles 2(1), 4(1), 7, 9(5), 14(3,6), 26).
6 To further underscore the importance of non-discrimination in human rights law: "The right of nondiscrimination is recognized in the Universal Declaration of Human Rights and across a multitude of treaties and national constitutions and laws, including the International Labor Organization Convention No. 169 Concerning Indigenous and Tribal Peoples in Independent Countries, the International Covenant on Civil and Political Rights, the International Convention on the Elimination of All Forms of

Racial Discrimination, the Conventional on the Elimination of all Forms of Discrimination against Women, and the Convention on the Rights of the Child. 123 States are obliged to protect human rights 'without any discrimination.'" – *Environmental Rule of Law, First Global Report*, 2019, Section 4, "Rights," p. 162.

7 Bridget Lewis, "Human Rights and Environmental Wrongs: Achieving Environmental Justice through Human Rights Law," *International Journal of Law Crime and Justice* 1(1) (2012). DOI: 10.5204/ijcjsd.v1i1.69. www.crimejusticejournal.com/article/view/676.

8 United States Environmental Protection Agency. 2015. Environmental Justice. Retrieved from www.epa.gov/environmentaljustice.

9 www.epa.gov/community-port-collaboration/environmental-justice-primer-ports-defining-environmental-justice (accessed 27-9-20).

10 "The right to be equal before the law (often referred to as 'nondiscrimination') and the rights of marginalized populations (and their members) require governments to apply environmental law in a manner that is nondiscriminatory and does not disadvantage those who rely on natural resources most heavily. These rights help protect women and children, who can be particularly vulnerable to environmental harms, and can give legal recourse to disadvantaged populations." – *Environmental Rule of Law, First Global Report*, 2019, Section 4, "Rights," pp. 161-162.

11 www.ohchr.org/en/professionalinterest/pages/crc.aspx.

12 Ibid.

13 "Courts in at least 12 countries have interpreted a constitutional right to life to include a right to a healthy environment in which to live that life." - *Environmental Rule of Law, First Global Report*, 2019, Section 4, "Rights," p. 163. https://wedocs.unep.org/bitstream/handle/20.500.11822/27381/ERL_ch4.pdf?sequence=1&isAllowed=y (accessed 4-10-20).

14 See also, Thomas A. Kerns and Kathleen Dean Moore, *Bearing Witness: The Human Rights Case Against Fracking and Climate Change*. Oregon: Oregon State University Press, 2021; chapter 2.1, "The Right to Life."

15 General comment No. 36 (2018) on article 6 of the International Covenant on Civil and Political Rights, on the right to life.

16 *Safe Climate: A Report of the Special Rapporteur on Human Rights and the Environment* (July 15, 2019) p. 18.

17 www.environmentandhumanrights.org/resources/udhr.pdf.

18 www.environmentandhumanrights.org/resources/ccpr.pdf.

19 Bridget Lewis, *Environmental Human Rights and Climate Change: Current Status and Future Prospects*. New York: Springer, 2008, p. 158.

20 Climate Change and Human Rights, United Nations Environment Programme, December 2015, pp. viii-10 (emphasis added). www.tribunalonfracking.org/wp-content/uploads/2015/06/UNEP-Climate-Chg-Hum-Rts-Report-12-10-15.pdf, p. 6.

21 *Understanding Human Rights and Climate Change*, Submission of the Office of the High Commissioner for Human Rights to the 21st Conference of the Parties to the United Nations Framework Convention on Climate Change,

11-26-15. www.tribunalonfracking.org/wp-content/uploads/2015/06/ UNHCHR-Understanding-HR-CC-COP21.pdf, pp. 2-19.

22 UNEP, Climate Change and Human Rights, 2015. www.tribunalonfracking. org/wp-content/uploads/2015/06/UNEP-Climate-Chg-Hum-Rts- Report-12-10-15.pdf; p. viii.

23 "The American Medical Association and the American College of Physicians recognised climate change as a health emergency in June 2019, and the British Medical Association the following month declared a climate emergency and committed to campaign for carbon neutrality by 2030.

The World Health Organisation has recognised since 2015 that climate change is the greatest threat to global health in the 21st century, and argued the scientific evidence for that assessment is 'overwhelming'." *The Guardian*, 9-3-19. www.theguardian.com/australia-news/2019/sep/03/australian-medical- association-declares-climate-change-a-health-emergency (accessed 10-19-20).

24 *The Guardian*, 9-3-19. www.theguardian.com/australia-news/2019/sep/03/ australian-medical-association-declares-climate-change-a-health-emergency (accessed 10-19-20).

25 "Effects of climate change on human health." https://en.wikipedia.org/ wiki/Effects_of_climate_change_on_human_health (accessed 10-19-20).

26 *Oregon Call to Action on Climate, Health and Equity*. 2-5-20. www.oregon publichealth.org/assets/Oregon%20CALL%20TO%20ACTION.pdf (accessed 2-15-20).

27 www.environmentandhumanrights.org/resources/udhr.pdf.

28 www.environmentandhumanrights.org/resources/cescr.pdf.

29 www.ohchr.org/en/professionalinterest/pages/crc.aspx.

30 www.environmentandhumanrights.org/resources/Aarhus%20convention. pdf.

31 www.environmentandhumanrights.org/resources/UN_Decl_on_Rts_of_ Indigenous_Peoples.pdf.

32 *Safe Climate: A Report of the Special Rapporteur on Human Rights and the Environment* (7-15-19) pp. 19-20.

33 www.environmentandhumanrights.org/resources/udhr.pdf.

34 www.environmentandhumanrights.org/resources/cescr.pdf.

35 www.ohchr.org/en/professionalinterest/pages/crc.aspx.

36 *Understanding Human Rights and Climate Change*, Submission of the Office of the High Commissioner for Human Rights to the 21st Conference of the Parties to the United Nations Framework Convention on Climate Change, 11-26-15. www.tribunalonfracking.org/wp-content/uploads/2015/06/UNHCHR- Understanding-HR-CC-COP21.pdf, pp. 2-19.

37 *Safe Climate: A Report of the Special Rapporteur on Human Rights and the Environment* (7-15-19) p. 20.

38 Lewis, *Environmental Human Rights and Climate Change*, p. 160.

39 Ibid., p. 161.

40 Associated Press, "Locust Outbreak, Most Serious in 25 Years, Hits East Africa," *Seattle Times*, 8-17-21. www.seattletimes.com/nation-world/theyre-back- trillions-of-locusts-descend-on-east-africa-in-second-wave/ (accessed 8-17-21).

41 See also, Kerns and Moore, *Bearing Witness*, chapter 2.2, "The Right to an Adequate Standard of Living."

42 *Understanding Human Rights and Climate Change*, Submission of the Office of the High Commissioner for Human Rights to the 21st Conference of the Parties to the United Nations Framework Convention on Climate Change, 11-26-15.   www.tribunalonfracking.org/wp-content/uploads/2015/06/UNHCHR-Understanding-HR-CC-COP21.pdf, pp. 2-19.

43 https://en.unesco.org/human-rights/water-sanitation (accessed 8-17-21).

44 www.environmentandhumanrights.org/resources/cedaw.pdf.

45 www.ohchr.org/en/professionalinterest/pages/crc.aspx.

46 www.environmentandhumanrights.org/resources/udhr.pdf.

47 www.environmentandhumanrights.org/resources/cescr.pdf.

48 *Understanding Human Rights and Climate Change*, Submission of the Office of the High Commissioner for Human Rights to the 21st Conference of the Parties to the United Nations Framework Convention on Climate Change, 11-26-15. www.tribunalonfracking.org/wp-content/uploads/2015/06/UNHCHR-Understanding-HR-CC-COP21.pdf, pp. 2-19.

49 Human Rights Watch, "There is no time left: climate change, environmental threats, and human rights in Turkana County, Kenya" (Human Rights Watch, 2015).

50 *Safe Climate: A Report of the Special Rapporteur on Human Rights and the Environment* (10-16-19) p. 21.

51 Lewis, *Environmental Human Rights and Climate Change*, p. 162.

52 "U.S. ratification of the Convention on the Rights of the Child," a Wikipedia article, discusses why some groups in the US have opposed ratification of this convention. https://en.wikipedia.org/wiki/U.S._ratification_of_the_Convention_on_the_Rights_of_the_Child.

53 Lauren, Paul Gordon, *The Evolution of International Human Rights*. Pennsylvania: University of Pennsylvania Press, 2nd ed, 2003, p. 249.

54 Convention on the Rights of the Child, Article 3,2. www.ohchr.org/en/professionalinterest/pages/crc.aspx

55 Ibid., Article 4.

56 Ibid., Article 12, 1.

57 Ibid., Article 12, 2.

58 This recognition from the Safe Climate report is important. Youth Climate Courts can serve as one more tool for youth who "are increasingly outspoken about the impacts of climate change on their rights and their future and the need for urgent action." While YCCs provide a tool for speaking truth to power and exerting effective agency, they also leave plenty of room for adaptation to local circumstances and the judgment of the organizing team.

59 A/HRC/35/13.

60 *Safe Climate: A Report of the Special Rapporteur on Human Rights and the Environment* (October 16, 2019) p. 22.

61 American Convention on Human Rights, entered into force 7-18-78. www.environmentandhumanrights.org/resources/American%20Convention%20on%20Human%20Rights.pdf.

62 General recommendation No. 37 on gender-related dimensions of disaster risk reduction in the context of climate change and A/HRC/41/26.

63 United Nations Development Programme (UNDP), *Gender Equality in National Climate Action: Planning for Gender- Responsive Nationally Determined Contributions* (UNDP 2016).

64 Center for International Environmental Law and Global Initiative for Economic, Social and Cultural Rights, *States' Human Rights Obligations in the Context of Climate Change: 2019 Update* (Center for International Environmental Law and Global Initiative for Economic, Social and Cultural Rights, 2019).

65 General recommendation No. 27 on older women and general recommendation No. 34 on the rights of rural women.

66 WHO, Gender, climate change and health (WHO, 2014).

67 Permanent Forum on Indigenous Issues, "Climate change and indigenous peoples" (Permanent Forum on Indigenous Issues, 2008).

68 CRPD/C/SYC/CO1.

69 *Safe Climate: A Report of the Special Rapporteur on Human Rights and the Environment* (July 15, 2019) pp. 23-24.

70 *Environmental Rule of Law, First Global Report*, 2019, Section 4, "Rights," p. 165. https://wedocs.unep.org/bitstream/handle/20.500.11822/27381/ERL_ch4.pdf?sequence=1&isAllowed=y (accessed 10-4-20).

71 www.environmentandhumanrights.org/resources/UN_Decl_on_Rts_of_Indigenous_Peoples.pdf.

72 www.environmentandhumanrights.org/resources/UN_Decl_on_Rts_of_Indigenous_Peoples.pdf.

73 www.environmentandhumanrights.org/resources/UN_Decl_on_Rts_of_Indigenous_Peoples.pdf.

74 The Inter-American Court of Human Rights, in *Mayagna (Sumo) Awas Tingni Community v Nicaragua* (2001). Quoted in Lewis, *Environmental Human Rights and Climate Change*, p. 28.

75 See also, Kerns and Moore, *Bearing Witness*, chapter 2.3, "The Right of Indigenous Peoples to Own, Use, Develop, and Control Traditional Lands and Resources."

76 *Environmental Rule of Law, First Global Report*, 2019, Section 4, "Rights," pp. 154-156. https://wedocs.unep.org/bitstream/handle/20.500.11822/27381/ERL_ch4.pdf?sequence=1&isAllowed=y (accessed 10-4-20).

77 A/HRC/40/55. https://documents-dds-ny.un.org/doc/UNDOC/GEN/G19/002/54/PDF/G1900254.pdf?OpenElement (accessed 8-17-21).

78 *Safe Climate: A Report of the Special Rapporteur on Human Rights and the Environment* (July 15, 2019) pp. 22-23.

79 "Convention on Access to Information, Public Participation in Decision-making and Access to Justice in Environmental Matters," June 25, 1998, Aarhus, Denmark, at www.environmentandhumanrights.org/resources/Aarhus%20convention.pdf

80 www.tribunalonfracking.org/judges-statements/.

81 http://permanentpeoplestribunal.org/wp-content/uploads/2019/04/AO-final-12-APRIL-2019.pdf, pp. 31-32. The Declaration on Human Rights and Climate Change is included as an Appendix to this book.

82 Climate Change and Human Rights, United Nations Environment Programme, December 2015, pp. viii–10. www.tribunalonfracking.org/wp-content/uploads/2015/06/UNEP-Climate-Chg-Hum-Rts-Report-12-10-15.pdf.

83 *Juliana v. United States*, no. 6:15-cv-01517-TC, 2016, p. 32, at https://static1.squarespace.com/static/571d109b04426270152febe0/t/5824e85e6a49638292ddd1c9/1478813795912/order+MTd.aiken.pdf.

84 Preamble of the United States Constitution: "We the People of the United States, in Order to form a more perfect Union, establish Justice, insure domestic Tranquility, provide for the common defence, promote the general Welfare, and secure the Blessings of Liberty to ourselves and our Posterity, do ordain and establish this Constitution for the United States of America."

85 www.youthclimatecourts.org/resources-for-ycc-planning/.

86 http://hrlibrary.umn.edu.

87 www.environmentandhumanrights.org/resources/udhr.pdf.

88 www.ohchr.org/en/professionalinterest/pages/crc.aspx.

89 www.environmentandhumanrights.org/resources/cedaw.pdf.

90 www.environmentandhumanrights.org/resources/UN_Decl_on_Rts_of_Indigenous_Peoples.pdf.

91 http://srenvironment.org/report/a-safe-climate-human-rights-and-climate-change (accessed 1-28-20).

92 www.tribunalonfracking.org/wp-content/uploads/2015/06/UNHCHR-Understanding-HR-CC-COP21.pdf.

93 www.tribunalonfracking.org/wp-content/uploads/2015/06/UNEP-Climate-Chg-Hum-Rts-Report-12-10-15.pdf.

Coda

Youth interventions for an addicted world

Society's heavy and increasing use of fossil fuels – despite those fuels' documented harms and despite persistent science-based calls for reducing their use – is recognized by many as a kind of societal addiction, an addiction of society itself. This societal addiction bears many resemblances to addictions with which individuals struggle.

Standard descriptions of personal addiction, that is, addiction of individual persons, typically characterize it as entailing a felt compulsive and chronic need for the habit-forming substance or activity despite that substance's or activity's harmful physical, psychological, or social consequences for oneself or others. The addicted individual often tries to quit using but just cannot seem to make it happen. He or she instead ends up using more and more of the substance to which they are addicted. This is how it is with a social entity's addiction too. The social entity knows that its using is causing harm to itself and others, maybe tries to quit or "cut back," but instead just keeps using more and more.

Imagine an individual addict asking their counselor whether they might be addicted to a certain substance. The counselor might ask,

> Have you sometimes thought about cutting down or controlling your use? Have you ever tried to cut down or control your use, but it just didn't work? Have you continued to use even against your better judgment and even though there have been negative consequences to your health, job, or family?

Affirmative answers to those questions signal the presence of an addiction.

Now imagine a social entity, like a nation for example, going to its experts and asking similar questions about its overuse of fossil fuels. Is the entity aware of the damage its using is causing? Has the entity ever thought about cutting back on its using, maybe even tried to, but just

DOI: 10.4324/9781003217640-5

has not been able to? Has the entity continued to use, even increased its usage, despite all the negative consequences to its people and families and environment? Affirmative answers to those questions signal the presence of an addiction.

If the individual's addiction continues to worsen, if it causes more and more damage and disarray in the addict's life and in the lives of people around them, then family, friends, and workmates may begin to wonder if the time has finally arrived to conduct a formal intervention. In just the same way, as a social entity's addiction to fossil fuels continues unabated, concerned citizens are beginning to seriously ask if the time has finally come to conduct a formal intervention. Young people and the Youth Climate Courts they organize can serve exactly that function: a necessary, life-saving, formal intervention to save the addicted social communities they love.

David Boyd, United Nations Special Rapporteur on Human Rights and the Environment, in his 2019 *Safe Climate* report, says it straight: "Society is addicted to fossil fuels. Despite 27 years of commitments dating back to the United Nations Framework Convention on Climate Change." He continues,

> the world is neither headed in the right direction, nor addressing the crisis at an adequate pace. Since 1990, global energy consumption has increased by 57 per cent. The share of the world's total energy supply provided by fossil fuels has remained unchanged at 81 per cent. Coal use is up 68 per cent, oil use is up 36 per cent and natural gas use is up 82 per cent. Even the fossil fuel share of electricity production has increased, from 62 per cent in 1992 to 65 per cent in 2016. Global greenhouse gas emissions are up 60 per cent since 1990. Wealthy people and large corporations are deeply invested in the status quo and use their immense economic and political power to resist the societal transformations needed to successfully address climate change.[1]

We all know that when an individual person is addicted to a substance, their use of that substance tends to increase over time. Dr Boyd shows here that the same pattern happens when a social entity is addicted to fossil fuels.

If we step back for a moment and look at the larger pattern of how an individual's addiction to a chemical substance develops, we will see virtually identical analogues to the way a social entity's addiction develops. We see, for example, that when an individual or a social body is first introduced to a new chemical, that chemical can initially prove very powerful at accomplishing its purpose and can seem, to all appearances, to be all upside and no downside. This was certainly the circumstance with opioid pain medications in the case of individuals, for example, and with chemical pesticides, synthetic plastics, and fossil fuels in the case of social entities.

When Sigmund Freud, for example, first began using cocaine, he found that it seemed to work wonders in increasing his energy, acuity, and productivity.[2] Only later, with continued and increasing usage, did the deep biological and psychological destruction start to become clinically evident. Many addictions begin with a period like that – sometimes shorter, sometimes longer – with an experience of successful pain relief, for example, or of accomplishment, capability, and power. Only at some later point is it discovered that, while the successes felt large and real in the beginning, with time and continued use those effects diminish and something ominous begins to happen. This beneath-the-surface sense of damage may not have been evident in the first flushes of success, may indeed not have made any appearance at all, and may not even have existed at that point. And yet with time, with continued use, with continued reliance on the new substance, and with the strengthening of habit and dependence, the downside effects begin to emerge, slowly at first, then faster and faster. We may try to not think about the downsides. We may willfully choose to avoid thinking about the destructiveness as long as we can, but eventually real damage is done and the harms of using become increasingly and insistently evident.

Unfortunately, by the time awareness of the damage does finally force itself into consciousness, some unavoidably strong, deep, and powerful personal habits have already taken root. The individual, or the social entity, has developed a web of daily practices, life-habits, social structures, and even life-beliefs that have come to feel normal and necessary. In a word, the addicted individual or social entity has developed a dependence on the substance. Use of the substance has worked its way deep into all the intersecting patterns and substructures of life, and is now experienced as a need. Quitting seems impossible. It has been tried and it just has not worked. It feels like there is no practical way up from what feels like abject despair.

When no realistic, feasible way forward looks remotely possible, things seem hopeless. That is when a well-planned, gentle, insistent, caring, forcefully direct, and powerful intervention can make all the difference to the addicted person. The addict usually does know, perhaps only at some dark quasi-conscious level, that their using needs to end and that, in fact, they desperately *want* it to end.

And yet, when that intervention does finally happen it can initially feel to the desperate addict like the intervenors are opposing them, fighting them, interfering with their needs, not helping them and definitely not "on their side." Yet in some deep way, the addict also knows, just as the intervenors do, that the addiction is out of control and the addict desperately needs help. Such an intervention, difficult, challenging and painful as it often is, can turn out to be what ultimately saves that addict's life. Months or years later, the recovering addict may feel deep gratitude to the family and friends who loved them enough to apply that pressure, forcing them to do what they themselves had long known they needed to do.

For a social entity too, introduction to a new substance can initially feel wonderful, as if it is all upside and no downside. In the case of fossil fuels, this all-upside-and-no-downside perspective lasted for many decades, perhaps for most of a century before the all too serious health impacts, environmental impacts, human rights impacts, and climate impacts started to become so abundantly clear.

By the time societies recognized the downsides, though, whole economic, political, and social structures had been built up that relied on those fuels, chemicals, and plastics. The initially immense upsides, unparalleled in human history, made it easy for societies to overlook, or deliberately ignore, the downsides of fossil fuel extraction and usage. Some policymakers may even have calculated that the adverse health impacts, the increased mortality, and social inequities experienced by a certain percentage of the population were simply an unfortunate but necessary social cost if societies were to enjoy the new benefits. These policymakers may have made the same moral calculation as those who *stayed* in Omelas, in Ursula LeGuin's famous little short story, "The Ones Who Walked Away from Omelas."[3] (LeGuin's story imagines a community, Omelas, in which the happy bliss of the community's members depends on the horrendous suffering of one small child, then explores the justness of such an arrangement.)

At some point in the social entity's addiction, though, the downsides become much too obvious to ignore. The climate impacts, the health impacts, the ecosystem and species-loss impacts simply become too publicly evident to ignore, especially when those downsides threaten to destroy all the upsides as well. This seems to be the point the world's governments are approaching now.

It is at exactly this point in a personal addiction that a planned intervention by caring family, friends, and workmates can be powerfully clarifying and effective. A young child tearfully confronting their alcoholic or drug-addled father, begging him to please, please stop, please go to treatment: "If you won't do it for my sake, then please at least do it for your own." A powerful, love-inspired intervention like that can truly make all the difference.

Because governments are the primary organs of formal policy-making in societies, it is governments, especially local governments, that will need the interventions by these young, caring, insistent, and organized Youth Climate Courts. The Youth Courts can caringly, directly, pointedly, and unambiguously clarify the issues for their government. They can exert pressure, tough love pressure, on local governments that have so far failed to enact the necessary policies and laws to guide their communities into a healthy future.

Thus, the young people who organize these Youth Climate Court trials are performing an intervention on behalf of the people, communities, and planet they love. The local governments in these communities may already realize that they need to make big changes, but so far most just have not done so. Governments, like people, can sometimes just get stuck and find themselves unable to imagine any realistic, workable way forward ... until they are forced to. In today's climate crisis, Youth Climate Court interventions can provide that extra measure of moral force a government needs to begin making the changes it has not, until now, known how to do.

So the test now is whether the intervention work done by these caring young people and their Youth Climate Courts will be effective in confronting our social addiction and whether local governments will take the message as seriously as their young people do.

. . . .

When good, concerned young leaders discover this Youth Climate Court option and find it intriguing, they may decide that they want to give it a go. They may feel excited by the idea, enlivened and empowered, and recognize it as a new and powerful way for them to speak their truth with a public voice and to exercise real, genuine, efficacious agency, providing a sincere, urgent, and much-needed intervention in a crisis that is already impacting, and will continue to dramatically impact, their lives so directly.

And when good, caring city mayors and council members, and county boards of commissioners, find themselves and their governments summoned to participate in a Youth Climate Court, they will realize how important it is for them to not offhandedly dismiss what young people are asking of them, as a fearful addict might want to do, but to instead engage respectfully and caringly in the important intervention work the Youth Climate Court is courageously undertaking. Local governments will hopefully realize, too, how crucially important it is that they respond with grace and generosity, grateful to the youth organizers for the genuineness, care, and passion they bring to their intervention work. It will be essential that elected officials encourage and give full respect to the young organizers and to the well-meaning intervention work they are struggling to accomplish. Smart elected officials will recognize right away how truly valuable these Youth Climate Courts can be for them and will welcome them and their organizers as allies in the hard work of governing in our desperately climate-challenged world.

Notes

1 David Boyd, United Nations Special Rapporteur on Human Rights and the Environment, *Safe Climate* report, p. 13.
2 Howard Markel, *An Anatomy of Addiction: Sigmund Freud, William Halsted, and the Miracle Drug Cocaine*. New York: Vintage, 2011.
3 For a link to Ursula LeGuin's "The Ones Who Walked Away from Omelas," and a discussion of its moral implications, see the *Classics of Science Fiction* article at https://classicsofsciencefiction.com/2020/04/11/a-philosophical-conversation-between-two-short-stories/.

Appendices

Appendix I: The Declaration on Human Rights and Climate Change

The Declaration on Human Rights and Climate Change can be useful to Youth Climate Court organizers in many ways, partly because it so clearly draws on existing, already-endorsed human rights declarations, covenants and conventions, and articulates their clear relevance for the climate crisis, partly because it so clearly recognizes the essential interwovenness between the rights of humans and the rights of Earth's other living beings and systems, and partly because it is so eminently quotable.

The 24 principles of the Declaration are divided into three parts:

I   Substantive rights, some of which apply primarily to human beings and others to "human beings, animals and living systems."

II   Procedural rights (which are absolutely essential for securing the substantive rights). These rights apply to human beings in their capacity as learners, communicators, and agents who can effect change.

III   Duties, which apply to persons, states, and "all parties." This includes governments at all levels, private businesses, corporations, banks, trusts, and other corporate and civil society entities such as schools, places of worship, non-governmental organizations, and so on.

The first draft of this Declaration was initiated by the Global Network for the Study of Human Rights and the Environment and prepared by a team of 13 scholars from seven different countries spread across five continents. The draft was completed in November 2015, to be made available for the COP21 meetings in Paris that year.

The draft was later submitted for review globally in nine European, African and Asian languages (Spanish, German, Italian, Polish, Norwegian,

Amharic, Mandarin, Persian and English) to environmental and human rights scholars, lawyers, jurists, indigenous community representatives, NGOs and others. Well over 100 thoughtful responses and suggestions were received in response to this review process and incorporated into the final draft.

The final version of the Declaration, completed in May 2016, was authorized by the drafting group for distribution.

Members of the drafting group:

ANNA GREAR, Professor of Law and Theory, Director of the GNHRE, Cardiff Law School, Wales, UK.

LOUIS J. Kotzé, Research Professor, North-West University, South Africa; Deputy-Director, GNHRE.

DR TOM KERNS, Director, Environment and Human Rights Advisory; Professor Emeritus of Philosophy, North Seattle College, USA.

DR KIRSTEN DAVIES, Senior Lecturer, Macquarie Law School, Macquarie University, Australia.

DR SAM ADELMAN, Associate Professor of Law, School of Law, University of Warwick, UK.

DEVA PRASAD M., Assistant Professor of Law, National Law School of India University, Bangalore, India.

JOSHUA C. GELLERS, Assistant Professor of Political Science and Public Administration, University of North Florida, USA.

DR KERRI WOODS, Lecturer in Political Theory, University of Leeds, UK.

ENGOBO EMESEH, Senior Lecturer in Law, Aberystwyth University, UK.

CATHERINE IORNS MAGALLANES, Senior Lecturer in Law, Victoria University of Wellington, New Zealand.

DR JOHN PEARSON, LLB. LLM. LLM. Lecturer in Environmental Law and Human Rights, University of Manchester, UK.

RAVI RAJAN, Professor, Department of Environmental Studies, University of California, Santa Cruz, USA.

DR. SILJA KLEPP, Senior Researcher/Acting Managing Director, Sustainability Research Center, University of Bremen, Germany.

Further information about the origins, structure and purposes of the DHRCC is available in "'The Declaration on Human Rights and Climate Change': A New Legal Tool for Global Policy Change," Kirsten Davies, et al., *Journal of Human Rights and the Environment* (8.2) September 2017,[1] and at the website of the Global Network for the Study of Human Rights and the Environment, www.gnhre.org.

Preamble

Guided by the United Nations Charter; The Universal Declaration of Human Rights; The International Covenant on Economic, Social and Cultural Rights; The International Covenant on Civil and Political Rights; The United Nations Declaration on the Rights of Indigenous Peoples; The Convention on the Elimination of All Forms of Discrimination against Women; The Vienna Declaration and Program of Action of the World Conference of Human Rights; The Universal Declaration on Rights of Children; The Draft United Nations Declaration on the Rights of Peasants; The International Labour Organization Convention No. 169; The 2030 Sustainable Development Goals; The Universal Declaration of the Rights of Mother Earth; The Earth Charter; The Nagoya Protocol; Title II of the 2008 Constitution of Ecuador, and other relevant international rights instruments,

Guided by The Stockholm Declaration of the United Nations Conference on the Human Environment; The United Nations Framework Convention on Climate Change, its Kyoto Protocol and the Paris Agreement; The World Charter for Nature; The United Nations Convention on the Law of the Sea; The Rio Declaration on Environment and Development, and other relevant instruments of international environmental law,

Reaffirming the universality, indivisibility, interdependence and interrelationality of all human rights, the interrelationality of all life on Earth and the dependency of all life on Earth on a healthy biosphere and Earth system integrity,

Recognizing that climate change, caused by the human industrial and consumer activities, disproportionally affects indigenous peoples, the poor, women and children, the vulnerable, small island and low elevation coastal communities, developing countries, least developed countries, future generations and innumerable living beings and systems,

Recognizing that the ultimate realization of human rights in the age of climate crisis requires the full legal protection of the living beings and systems upon which human life depends,

Recognizing that human beings are part of the living Earth system,

Recognizing the climate destructive and ecocidal results of assuming human separation from nature,

Recognizing the need for all cultures, faiths and traditions to play a role in the fullest development of climate and environmental stewardship, the teaching of respect for all living beings and systems and the development of climate resilient communities,

Recognizing that science confirms the threats of climate change to the Earth's systems and its multiple life forms,

Recognizing that science confirms the threat of climate change to the livelihoods and well-being of present and future generations,

Recognizing that climate impacts disproportionally affect innumerable living beings and systems that are intrinsically valuable in their own right and unable to defend themselves,

Recognizing that climate change displaces populations and that international, cross-border and internal migration has increased due to climate change and is likely to continue to do so,

Recognizing that courts and jurists of international standing link the fulfillment of human rights to a secure, healthy and ecologically viable environment, and consequently recognize that harming the environment undermines human rights,

Recognizing that it is the stewardship responsibility of human beings to respond to the climate harms and damage caused by human activities,

Deeply concerned by the severe human rights consequences of the continuing political failure to reach adequate commitments on climate mitigation and adaptation; by the dominance of the market as the primary value coordinating international responses to the climate crisis; and by the ongoing lack of accountability for corporate actors that violate human, environmental and climate rights,

Convinced that the potential irreversibility of climate change effects gives rise to an urgent need for new forms of state and non-state responsibility, accountability and liability.

The following principles are declared

I

1   Human rights and a profound commitment to climate justice are interdependent and indivisible.

2   All human beings, animals and living systems have the right to a secure, healthy and ecologically sound Earth system.

3   All human beings have the right to fairness, equity and justice in all climate resilience, adaptation and mitigation measures and efforts.

4   All human beings have the right to a planetary climate suitable to meet equitably the ecologically responsible needs of present generations without impairing the rights of future generations to meet equitably their ecologically responsible needs.

5   All human beings, animals and living systems have the right to the highest attainable standard of health, free from environmental

pollution, degradation and harmful emissions and to be free from dangerous anthropogenic interference with the climate system such that rising global temperatures are kept well below 1.5 degrees centigrade above preindustrial levels.

6 All human beings have the right to investments in adaptation and mitigation to prevent the deleterious consequences of anthropogenic climate change, and to international solidarity and timely assistance in the event of climate change driven catastrophes.

7 All human beings, animals and living systems have the right to fairness, equity and justice in respect of responses to the threat of climate change. This includes protection from deleterious impacts caused by adaptation and mitigation efforts to develop climate resilience, and by the potential deployment of climate geoengineering technologies.

8 All human beings have the right to a just transition toward a sustainable society characterized by meaningful inclusion and distributive justice.

II

9 All human beings have the right to information about, and to participation in, decision-making processes related to alterations made to the physical environments they rely upon for their health and survival.

10 All human beings have the right to information concerning the climate. The information shall be timely, clear, understandable and available without undue financial burden to the applicant.

11 All human beings have the right to hold and express opinions and to disseminate ideas and information regarding the climate.

12 All human beings have the right to climate and human rights education. This education includes the right to learn from multiple perspectives and to understand non-human natural modes of behavior and the requirements of flourishing planetary ecosystems.

13 All human beings have the right to active, free, and meaningful participation in planning and decision-making activities and processes that may have an impact on the climate. This particularly includes the rights of indigenous peoples, women and other under-represented groups to equality of meaningful participation. This includes the right to a prior assessment of the climate and human rights consequences of proposed actions. This includes the right to equality of hearing and the right for processes to be free of domination by powerful economic actors. This includes the rights of indigenous peoples to participate in

the protection of their rights to their lands, territories, natural resources, tenure rights and cultural heritage.

14 All human beings have the right to associate freely and peacefully with others, and to gather peacefully in public spaces, for purposes of protecting the climate or the rights of those affected by climate harm.

15 All human beings have the right to effective remedies and redress in administrative or judicial proceedings for climate harm or the threat or risk of such harm, including modes of compensation, monetary or otherwise.

III

16 All persons, individually and in association with others, have a moral responsibility to avoid and/or to minimize practices known to contribute to climate damage.

17 All States and business enterprises have a duty to protect the climate and to respect the rights set out in this Declaration.

18 All Parties shall, in all climate change-related actions, respect, protect, promote, and fulfill the rights of indigenous peoples. Such rights include support to facilitate mitigation measures; rights to collective self-determination and to free, prior, and informed consent; to full and equal participation in environmental and political processes; and to respect and protection for indigenous traditional knowledge. This shall include respect and protection for indigenous customary laws, and proper recognition of the role of indigenous peoples in ensuring the integrity and resilience of natural ecosystems.

19 All Parties shall, in all climate change-related actions, ensure gender equality and the full and equal participation of women; intergenerational equity; a just transition of the workforce that creates decent work; food sovereignty; and the integrity and resilience of natural ecosystems.

20 All States have a duty to provide assistance and solidarity to climate refugees. States shall respect the rights to assistance and solidarity and create the necessary legal frameworks to assist and support climate refugees in order to ensure their life and dignity.

21 All States shall respect and ensure the right to a secure, healthy and ecologically sound environment and to a stable climate, and ensure the rights outlined in Parts I-III of this Declaration. Accordingly, they shall adopt the administrative, legislative, and other measures necessary to effectively implement the rights in this Declaration.

22 All States shall ensure international cooperation with other States and international organizations and agencies for the purpose of respecting the rights outlined in Parts I-III of this Declaration. All States shall observe the rights and duties in this Declaration, including extraterritorially.

23 All international organizations and agencies shall observe the rights and duties in this Declaration, including the human and procedural rights of indigenous peoples, women, and other traditionally under-represented and marginalized groups and individuals.

24 All States, international organizations, business enterprises, and individuals acting to reduce climate harms shall respect and recognize the rights of any affected human beings and other living beings and systems to be free from climate change-related harm.

For more information and to endorse this Declaration, please visit www.gnhre.org.

Appendix II: The *Restorative Justice Only* option

The focus of this book has been to describe how and why Youth Climate Courts can organize and conduct trials of their local governments. It has described how, if that government is found guilty of not adequately doing its part to protect people's rights, the Youth Court will issue one or more mandates requiring the government to begin doing more to meet its human rights obligations. One version of that mandate, as described above, would require the government to enter into a restorative justice process with the Youth Court. It would require that the youth and government both meet together with a restorative justice facilitator, each listen attentively to the other's concerns, and then together work out what the government's next steps should be to "put things right" with respect to its climate obligations. The primary goal is for the two parties to hear each other, understand each other to some degree, and then figure out how best to heal or ameliorate the harm that was done. As Howard Zehr explains in *The Little Book of Restorative Justice*, the goal of the whole restorative justice process is "to provide an experience of healing for all concerned."[2] In this Youth Climate Court model, the mandate is issued and the restorative justice process begins only *after* that government has been found guilty and after it has been required by the court to "make amends" for its negligence.

But suppose that the Youth Courts, instead of proceeding immediately to trial, were to meet directly with the City Council, County Board of Commissioners, or other governing body ahead of time and propose the restorative justice process right from the start, before conducting a trial? This could potentially be a somewhat friendlier and less contentious approach and, if the local government body is willing to commit to the process, perhaps as effective. (The option of the Youth Court conducting a trial later could always be held in abeyance if the government proves insufficiently cooperative.)

There may be a case in which a local government body has already realized and publicly acknowledged that it has not done enough to address the climate crisis and that it has failed to live up to its human rights obligations in that regard. How might a government body have come to realize that? Perhaps they are simply a well-informed, knowledgeable and morally responsible government. Or perhaps the Youth Climate Court has informally, in person or in writing, presented that government with clear information and persuasive arguments that have convincingly demonstrated to that government what the climate crisis and human rights obligations require of them.

In the case of a friendly, well-disposed, and well-informed local government like that, it might be possible for the Youth Court to instead make a direct, friendly request to that government, right up front, to commit its members to learning about their government's human rights obligations as described in this book and elsewhere, and entering into a formal restorative justice process with the young people and with a trained restorative justice facilitator. If a truly genuine commitment were forthcoming from members of that government, then the members of the Youth Climate Court team would serve, throughout the process, as representatives of both themselves and the community.

It would, though, take the strong commitment of a genuinely caring, serious, well-informed and human rights-responsible government body for this "Restorative Justice Only" process to be effective. It may also require some level of a prior friendly relationship between the Youth Court organizers and members of that government. With a serious commitment and good will on the part of both parties, the Restorative Justice Only approach may turn out to be effective in some cases. As for outcomes, this process too, of course, would need to result in a science-based and human rights-respecting plan for how that government will do its part to meet its climate and human rights obligations to the satisfaction of the Youth Climate Court organizers.

And, as a last resort, if the "Restorative Justice Only" process turned out to not be effective, the Youth Climate Court organizers would always have the option of initiating a Youth Climate Court trial as described above.

Appendix III: A note on Rights of Nature

Human rights norms serve as the grounding for Youth Climate Courts for all the reasons we have seen, including the fact that governments do already have recognized human rights obligations and can thus be called to account if they do not adequately meet those obligations. In only a few countries, however, have governments recognized that they bear any formal rights obligations to the natural world. That means that the prospect of Youth Climate Court organizers basing an entire trial only on a government's duty to meet its rights-of-nature obligations may not be a workable strategy in most countries.

On the other hand, there may be some venues in which it would be far too limiting if the trial's arguments were based only on the *human* rights side of things without also recognizing the nature's rights perspective. The rights-of-nature perspective properly acknowledges the inherent value of the planet's other living beings and systems and recognizes that those beings and systems are also rights-bearing beings and have value beyond their mere utility for human purposes. Not including that perspective in the prosecution's arguments could be problematic in some trial venues, because it would exclude the recognition of human beings as part of nature, rather than somehow outside of, or above, nature.[3]

When issuing their Advisory Opinion in the 2018 Permanent Peoples' Tribunal Session on Human Rights, Fracking and Climate Change,[4] the judges recognized the importance of nature's rights as well as human rights, in what they termed a "blended jurisprudence." The blended jurisprudence they recommend sees human rights and nature's rights as complementary rather than oppositional. A recent United Nations report agrees: "The ecosystem and other beings have value and importance beyond their use or benefit to humans,"[5] and this should be acknowledged.

In some specific venues, then, Youth Climate Courts may want to include in their arguments the recognition that nature too has rights. *Human* rights will still be the central focus and ground of the prosecutor's arguments in Youth Climate Court trials, largely because governments do already have recognized obligations to respect and protect the rights of their human citizens. It is also true that human rights standards are already well established in law while the development of nature's rights law is still nascent and developing.

For those interested in incorporating rights-of-nature arguments into their prosecutorial arguments, the following resources may be especially helpful.

- Australian Earth Laws Alliance, Michelle Maloney, director[6]
- Ecological Law and Governance Association[7]
- Earth Law Alliance, Lisa Mead, director[8]
- Universal Declaration of the Rights of Mother Earth[9]
- The Advisory Opinion of the Permanent Peoples' Tribunal Session on Human Rights, Fracking and Climate Change[10]
- Numerous books are available on the Rights of Nature but I will mention here only two:
  - *The Rights of Nature: A Legal Revolution That Could Save the World*, by David R. Boyd, ECW Press, 2017[11]
  - *Bearing Witness: The Human Rights Case Against Fracking and Climate Change*, by Thomas Kerns and Kathleen Dean Moore, Oregon State University Press, 2021. See especially chapter 3, "How Fracking and Climate Change Violate the Rights of Nature."[12]

Appendix IV: Measures that local governments should consider including in their Climate Action Plans

- Provide the public with accessible, affordable and understandable information regarding the causes and consequences of the global climate crisis;
- Incorporate climate change into the educational curriculum at all levels;
- Ensure an inclusive, equitable and gender-based approach to public participation in all climate-related actions, with a particular emphasis on empowering the most affected populations, namely women, children, young people, indigenous peoples and local communities, persons living in poverty, persons with disabilities, older persons, migrants, displaced people, and other potentially at-risk communities;
- Enable affordable and timely access to justice and effective remedies for all, to hold governments and businesses accountable;
- Assess the potential climate change and human rights impacts of all plans, policies, and proposals;
- Integrate gender equality into all climate actions, enabling women to hold leadership positions;
- Respect the rights of indigenous peoples in all climate actions, particularly their right to free, prior, and informed consent;
- Provide strong protection for environmental and human rights defenders working on all climate-related issues, from land use to fossil fuels; vigilantly protect defenders from harassment, intimidation and violence;

- Prepare a rights-based deep decarbonization plan to achieve net-zero-carbon emissions by 2050, in accordance with article 4, paragraph 19, of the Paris Agreement;
- Enact laws or policies that phase in zero-carbon transportation, including zero-emission vehicle mandates and low-carbon fuel standards;
- Reject any expansion of fossil fuel infrastructure;
- Accelerate actions to reduce short-lived climate pollutants (methane, black carbon, ground-level ozone and hydrofluorocarbons);
- Commit to ending deforestation by 2025 and immediately begin participating in the trillion tree reforestation program[13];
- Phase out the production and use of harmful single-use plastics by 2025, as plastic production generates high volumes of greenhouse gas emissions;
- Take steps to reduce emissions from aviation and shipping;
- Promote healthy, plant-based diets that are less land-, resource-, and greenhouse gas emission-intensive;
- Take action to substantially reduce food waste;
- Develop adaptation actions through inclusive, participatory processes, informed by the knowledge, aspirations and specific contexts of affected communities and individuals;
- Implement adaptation plans that address both extreme weather disasters and slow-onset events by building or upgrading infrastructure (such as water, sanitation, health and education facilities) to be climate resilient; by developing disaster risk reduction and management strategies, early warning systems and emergency response plans; and by providing disaster relief and humanitarian assistance in emergencies;
- Provide social protection mechanisms to reduce vulnerability to climate-related disasters and stresses, enabling people to become more resilient;
- Prioritize nature-based adaptation actions, because protecting and restoring ecosystems can reduce vulnerability, buffering the impacts of extreme weather disasters and slow-onset events, and enhance ecosystem services, including fresh water, clean air, fertile soil, pest control, and pollination;
- Accelerate and scale up actions to strengthen the resilience and adaptive capacity of food systems and people's livelihoods;
- Ensure that adaptation actions do not reduce the vulnerability of one group at the expense of other people, future generations or the environment;

- Consistently report on the extent to which this government is fulfilling its human rights obligations relating to climate change;
- Encourage businesses to respect their human rights responsibilities relating to climate change.

In addition, an excellent source of information about Climate Action Plans for local governments is available at The David Suzuki Foundation.[14]

Appendix V: Potential risks to youth organizers?

Might there be some risks for Youth Climate Court organizers as they plan and conduct their trial? Might they experience pressures or criticism from community members, from friends, from elected officials, from employers or employees at certain businesses, perhaps even from teachers or parents who disagree with their stance on the climate crisis or who disagree with their way of addressing it? Might they be harassed by impolite people or groups who strongly disagree with them?

To help reduce the likelihood of responses like these it may be best for most organizing teams to not make their efforts and plans publicly known until most of their preparatory work has already been completed and the organizing team feels confident about how the trial will proceed. Of course they will want to make their plans public early enough in the process to give the defendant government adequate time to respond and prepare, and also early enough to ensure adequate media coverage. But before going public, they will want to feel confident that they have talked through with each other and pre-planned how best to respond to any potentially troubling responses to their work.

Organizers might want to quietly ask ahead of time for support from trusted friends, teachers, and family members. That way their support people could stand up for them and support them should any unpleasantness occur from someone in the community, from local businesses, or from elected officials.

It will probably also be best to not disclose their decisions as to whom the jury members will be until the last minute, perhaps not until the trial begins. That way jurors will face less risk of being lobbied, pressured, bribed, or perhaps even threatened by people who would want to influence their vote. Some teams may choose to not ever disclose jurors' identities, leaving that decision up to individual jurors after the trial has been completed.

Notes

1 www.tribunalonfracking.org/wp-content/uploads/2019/03/JHRE-DHRCC-article-Davies.pdf.

2 Howard Zehr, *The Little Book of Restorative Justice: Revised and Updated*, Good Books, Kindle Edition, p. 22.

3 "Rights-based approaches can be limited by their focus on human beings and often solely on living human beings. As noted above, a human rights-based approach fails to acknowledge inherent rights in nature independent of anthropocentric values placed on resources and the environment. Moreover, historically, most human rights have focused on the rights of living individuals to a particular outcome. With growing recognition of the rights of future generations, this is slowly changing." – *Environmental Rule of Law, First Global Report*, 2019, Section 4, "Rights," pp. 137-182, p. 154.

4 See www.tribunalonfracking.org/judges-statements/ (accessed 12-27-19).

5 *Environmental Rule of Law, First Global Report*, 2019, Section 4, "Rights," p. 141. https://wedocs.unep.org/bitstream/handle/20.500.11822/27381/ERL_ch4.pdf?sequence=1&isAllowed=y (accessed 10-4-20).

6 www.earthlaws.org.au.

7 https://elgaworld.org.

8 https://earthlawyers.org.

9 www.eldis.org/document/A59434.

10 www.tribunalonfracking.org/judges-statements/.

11 www.amazon.com/Rights-Nature-Legal-Revolution-Could/dp/1770412395/ref=sr_1_2?dchild=1&keywords=boyd%2C+rights+of+nature&qid=1607126079&sr=8-2.

12 http://osupress.library.oregonstate.edu/book/bearing-witness.

13 https://onetreeplanted.org/blogs/stories/1-trillion-trees?ads_cmpid=9320902284&ads_adid=93132202286&ads_matchtype=b&ads_network=g&ads_creative=417618435552&utm_term=one%20trillion%20trees&ads_targetid=kwd-866424134520&utm_campaign=&utm_source=adwords&utm_medium=ppc&ttv=2&gclid=CjwKCAjwsNiIBhBdEiwAJK4khpF6Krv3bgAEo-krCMhz3pT0eYrCtDGq6Yl6IGjaUcmvQqdMO-vtjBoCIIAQAvD_BwE.

14 https://davidsuzuki.org/what-you-can-do/learn-about-climate-action-plans/.

For Product Safety Concerns and Information please contact our EU
representative GPSR@taylorandfrancis.com
Taylor & Francis Verlag GmbH, Kaufingerstraße 24, 80331 München, Germany